D1474246

CITY AND HINTERLAND

Recent Titles in Contributions in American History
Series Editor: Jon L. Wakelyn

Voting in Provincial America: A Study of Elections in the Thirteen Colonies, 1689-1776
Robert J. Dinkin

The French Forces in America, 1780-1783
Lee Kennett

Cold War Political Justice: The Smith Act, the Communist Party and American Civil Liberties
Michal R. Belknap

The Many-Faceted Jacksonian Era: New Interpretations
Edward Pessen, editor

Manning the New Navy: The Development of a Modern Naval Enlisted Force, 1899-1940
Frederick S. Harrod

Riot, Rout, and Tumult: Readings in American Social and Political Violence
Roger Lane and John J. Turner, Jr., editors

The Long Shadow: Reflections on the Second World War Era
Lisle A. Rose

The Politics of Wartime Aid: American Economic Assistance to France and French Northwest Africa, 1940-1946
James J. Dougherty

The Oil Cartel Case: A Documentary Study of Antitrust Activity in the Cold War Era
Burton I. Kaufman

Two Nations Over Time: Spain and the United States, 1776-1977
James W. Cortada

Farmers without Farms: Agricultural Tenancy in Nineteenth-Century Iowa
Donald L. Winters

The Mess in Washington: Manpower Mobilization in World War II
George Q. Flynn

ROBERTA BALSTAD MILLER

CITY AND HINTERLAND

A case study of urban growth and regional development

Contributions in American History, Number 77
GREENWOOD PRESS
WESTPORT, CONNECTICUT • LONDON, ENGLAND

Library of Congress Cataloging in Publication Data

Miller, Roberta Balstad.
City and hinterland.

(Contributions in American history; no. 77
ISSN 0084-9219)
Bibliography: p.
Includes index.
1. Cities and towns—Growth—United States.
2. Regional economics—History. 3 Regional
planning—United States—History. I. Title.
HT123.M538 301.36'1'0974765 78-55340
ISBN 0-313-20524-8

Library of Congress Catalog Card Number: 78-55340
ISBN: 0-313-20524-8
ISSN: 0084-9219

First published in 1979

Greenwood Press, Inc.
51 Riverside Avenue, Westport, Connecticut 06880

Printed in the United States of America

10 9 8 7 6 5 4 3 2 1

To my parents and to John

CONTENTS

TABLES

FIGURES

ACKNOWLEDGMENTS

I have benefited from the generosity and help of many people in the preparation of this book. John Modell was a stimulating adviser and provided valuable help on each expansion of the manuscript. Robert Swierenga, Charles Tilly, and Stephan Thernstrom read the entire manuscript and graciously provided useful commentary and suggestions. Donald C. Dahmann also offered helpful advice.

My work was made easier because of the assistance of a number of archivists and librarians, particularly Virginia Hawley of the Western Reserve Historical Society; Richard Wright of the Onondaga Historical Association; and Nancy L. Carmichael and Melanie Snyder of the Social Science Research Council's Center for Coordination of Research on Social Indicators. The staffs of the Syracuse Public Library; the George Arents Research Library, Syracuse University; the Department of Manuscripts and University Archives, Cornell University; and the Hiram College Library were also very helpful.

The maps and diagrams were prepared by Thomas Vonier. Helen Keefe, Ruth Ann Muller, and Susan Baghdadi typed various drafts of the manuscript. Hilda Rogan helped with the final preparation of the manuscript.

Financial assistance was provided through a Putnam D. McMillan Fellowship, a Graduate School Special Grant (University of Minnesota), and an Alice E. Smith Fellowship of the State Historical Society of Wisconsin.

My husband, Floyd J. Miller, read and reread every part of the manuscript, providing not only the valuable advice and commentary of both historian and editor, but also encouragement and support throughout the research and writing of the book. My son Aaron, whose birth coincided with the beginning of my interest in Onondaga County, provided a welcome diversion from my work.

Roberta Balstad Miller

CITY AND HINTERLAND

CHAPTER 1

Introduction

Although there is little doubt that urbanization and regional economic development have been intimately related in the growth of the United States, the nature of this nexus has seldom been explored with any depth. Scholars have produced excellent studies of the growth of specific cities, and examinations of both regional development and interregional economic relationships have an honorable historiographical tradition dating back to Frederick Jackson Turner's early work on frontier and section. Yet the study of American urban growth as an integral part of the development process of the surrounding region and, in turn, as a crucial influence upon that region has rarely been attempted. Concern over the impact of the hinterland on the city has been limited instead to studies of trade rivalries and of controversies among businessmen in various cities to control regional transportation routes, while the influence of the city on the hinterland has been examined largely in terms of the extension of national urban culture and technology to rural areas. In most cases, the history of the American city has been divorced from that of the broader region of which the city was a part.[1]

Nor has the interest in patterns of regional development among those in other fields been directed toward the evolution and development of cities and their hinterlands over time. The analysis of regional development has been focused upon contemporary development and change. Eric E. Lampard suggests, moreover, that neither the ahistorical micro-framework of location theory nor the nationally aggregated framework of most theory on regional economic growth can contribute to a developmental perspective on the growth of cities and their hinterlands.[2]

Part of the reason for the long neglect of the study of urban growth in the context of regional development in the United States has been the absence of an integrated development theory which recognizes the impact of national and subnational factors on local development. What studies of regional development there are have been based upon a hypothetical model of internal regional differentiation and growth. While logically consistent for a closed regional system, this model is inapplicable under the conditions of national expansion—physical, social, and economic—which affected all aspects of American life in the nineteenth century and prevented the formation of the closed regional systems so essential to the explanations of existing regional theory. City-regions in the United States did not begin with the isolated subsistence village economy that Johann Heinrich von Thünen described in *The Isolated State*, a book published in 1826 which marked the beginning of attempts to rationalize regional development. Nor did growing American settlements and their hinterlands experience well-developed intraregional trade prior to interregional trade, as economists Edgar M. Hoover and Joseph L. Fisher presuppose in their more recent synthesis of stages of regional development. Rather, American city-regions emerged out of the lateral expansion of the coastal economy—products of the westward movement which took place between the late 1780s and the end of the nineteenth century.[3]

The conjunction of an open frontier and an expanding population led to new patterns of regional development in the United States at this time. The large-scale migration westward coincided with a great increase in the nation's population and resulted in the simultaneous growth of both new and existing cities and regions as it also encouraged trade between these population centers. National influences affected cities and their hinterlands separately as well as the entire city-region as a unit. In terms of population change, for example, national migration currents provided new populations for the swelling cities and also carried residents of the urban hinterland outside the city-region to new homes in different areas.

In order to understand how national economic, technological, and social conditions shaped urban growth in the nineteenth century, we must examine the impact of these factors on the entire city-region. The study of cities alone provides an incomplete picture of urban development, for the growth of the city affects the development of the city's hinterland. The continuing interaction between the growing city and its hinterland has a further impact on both areas, as when, for example, the city draws upon the hinterland for business or new residents or the hinterland evolves in response to the changing role of the city in the regional economy. Yet we know little about the relationship between cities and their hinterlands, or changes in this relationship, over time.

Since only a broad knowledge of specific patterns of regional development can lead to theoretical formulations of general patterns of regional development, working hypotheses must be constructed from particular case studies. The following is such a study, an intensive examination of Onondaga County in central New York—including the city of Syracuse—from around 1790 to 1860. It should not be construed as a history of the county, and still less as a history of Syracuse. Rather, it is an analysis of the development of the city and its hinterland and the relationship between this city-region and the nation during a period of rapid urban growth.

Although economic regions can vary in size from areas as large as several states to areas as small as several townships, city-region or region, as used here, refers to a city and its hinterland. Hoover and Fisher have conceived of an economic region in terms of the larger definition, while Douglass North has defined an economic region as a somewhat smaller area which develops around a common export base; in practice, such regions generally include all or part of one or two states. However if region is used in the sense of city-region to refer to the city and its immediately surrounding hinterland, as it is in this study, the area included will be considerably smaller than a multi-state region. This small scale definition allows us to examine the impact of transportation and socioeconomic changes within the region and among the region's population much more closely than would be possible if a larger area were involved.[4]

In reality, the hinterland of a city is difficult to delineate, for a city has a different hinterland for each of the commercial products it distributes and the social and economic services it provides. Locating these hinterlands—even assuming that supporting data to determine their location could be found a century and a half later—would result in a series of unwieldy hinterland boundaries shifting constantly over time for each product and service. The only way these various hinterlands could be harmonized for analytical purposes would be to find the mean of these points in time and space; and even if the mean hinterland were defined, analysis over time would be difficult because of the impossibility of locating comparative data at a number of time points for such a composite region.[5]

In view of the difficulty in determining the true hinterland of a city, the county unit serves in this study as a convenient surrogate for the many functional hinterlands that actually existed. Defining a county as the hinterland of a city within its boundaries offers two advantages for a study of city-hinterland relationships. First, it is a bounded political area with inclusive census and legal records available over a long period of time, and second, the small scale of the county unit provides an area in which detailed analysis over time is feasible.

Given the decision to locate the city-region in a county unit, Onondaga County was chosen as the locus of this study because it offered a number of analytical advantages over other counties. All the major interregional transportation innovations of the early nineteenth century appeared in Onondaga County at an early point in their development. As a result, intraregional differentiation induced by shortening the travel time to interregional markets could be expected to appear earlier in this county than in other counties, and an analysis of the development of the county could illuminate the subsequent process of regional development in other parts of the United States in the nineteenth century. The mushrooming growth of the city of Syracuse in this period also meant that an examination of Onondaga County could provide an opportunity for studying changes in the relationship between a city and its hinterland during the transition from frontier to settled area and during a period of rapid urban growth. In addition, the city of Syracuse was located almost in the center of the county and at a dividing point between two distinct types of terrain, one very flat and the other quite hilly. This provided a county hinterland which both stretched out from the city in all directions and was likely to contain varied agricultural patterns, and it promised a more fruitful study than a county which composed a single, topographically uniform slice or portion of a city's hinterland.[6] (See Figure 1.)

The model of urban growth and regional development which emerges from this examination of Onondaga County in the late eighteenth century and the first half of the nineteenth century emphasizes the relationship between interregional transportation innovation, urban growth, and changes in trading patterns in the maturation of a frontier or underdeveloped area. Onondaga County, like other frontier areas at this time, was gradually settled by migrants from eastern settlements. The configuration of the original settlement of the county was related to existing transportation routes (and thus migration routes) and the social ties and economic contacts among migrants. Initial settlement patterns continued with little modification until the construction of the Erie Canal in the 1820s. The canal both shortened travel time between Onondaga County and the East and, because it was built along a more northerly route than the principal turnpike then in use, altered traffic patterns within the county. As a consequence, an interregional transportation innovation—the canal—led to a shift in existing migration and trading patterns which, in turn, led to the growth of the city of Syracuse. Transportation changes, the growth of the city, and alterations in trading patterns together affected contemporary agricultural and industrial activities and patterns of persistence and migration in the city's hinterland. This process is illustrated in Figure 2.

Transportation innovations thus played a primary role in setting in motion the chain of events that led to the growth of Syracuse and shaped the development of its hinterland in Onondaga County. This is not to say that cities like Syracuse were merely, in Lampard's words, "passive incidents in the growth and refinement of transportation systems." Rather, at a time when the United States was expanding in its physical size and its population, transportation innovations were a primary influence on the shape of that expansion. Although some of the changes that took place in Onondaga County after 1820, such as the growth of a regional

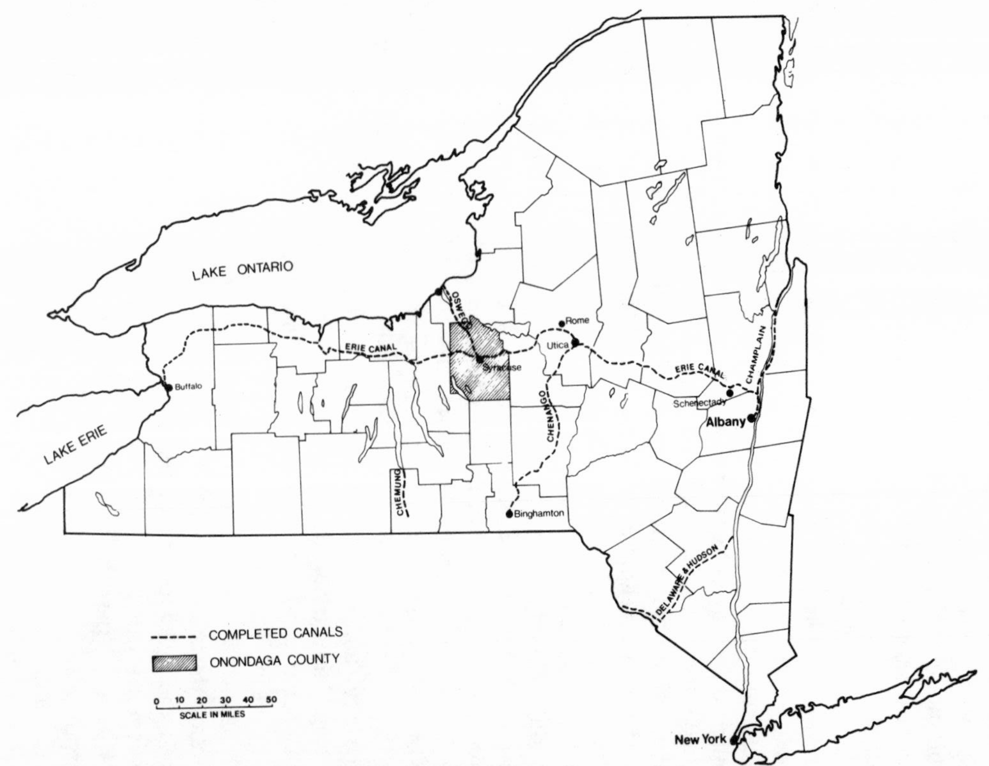

Figure 1. New York State, 1838

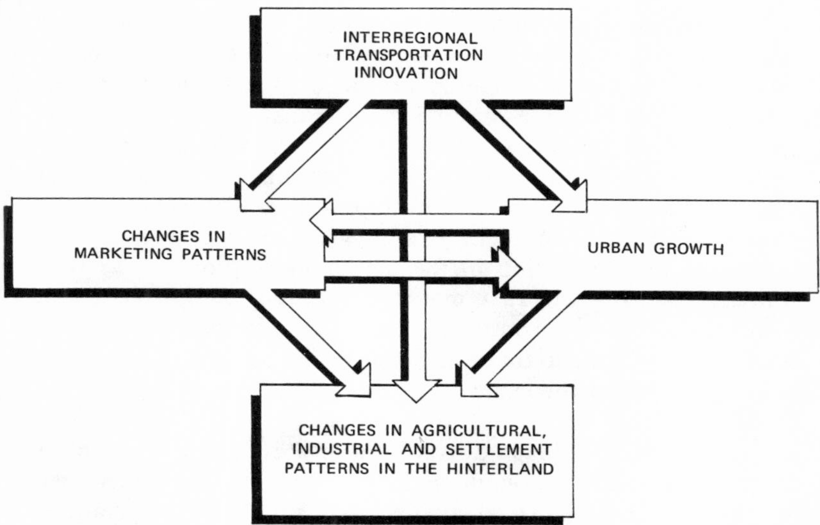

Figure 2. The Process of Change in Onondaga County, 1820-1840

marketing system and the urbanization of industrial activity, might have taken place without a major interregional transportation innovation such as the canal, the construction of the canal through Onondaga modified and eventually accelerated the course of these changes. Because the Erie Canal led directly to the growth of the city of Syracuse, its influence was crucial in structuring future development throughout the county.[7]

The Erie Canal serves a dual purpose in this study. It will be viewed not simply as a canal, possessing specific transport properties, but also as a prototype overland interregional transportation system, influential as the first transportation innovation inaugurated after the settlement of the county. This role could as easily have been played by another method of transportation, and, somewhat later, it was. The construction in the 1850s of the Binghamton and Syracuse Railroad through the southern part of Onondaga County resulted in the same changes there as were observed in central Onondaga at the time the Erie Canal was built.

Interregional transportation innovation was considerably less important in the region's development after the differentiation of Onondaga County into urban and rural components in the decade and a half following the opening of the canal. The course of the railroad, a second interregional transportation innovation, was determined by existing settlement and trading patterns and did not significantly alter the relationships among settlements in the county except in the southern townships. The role of interregional transportation innovation in the development process was thus transformed after the first major innovation. From exerting a dominant influence on intraregional differentiation over time, it became subordinate to the stronger forces it had created—namely, urban growth and the expanding interregional marketing system. (See Figure 3.)

The remainder of this study traces this process of development in Onondaga County by examining the differentiation of the frontier area into city and hinterland and delineating the changing relation-

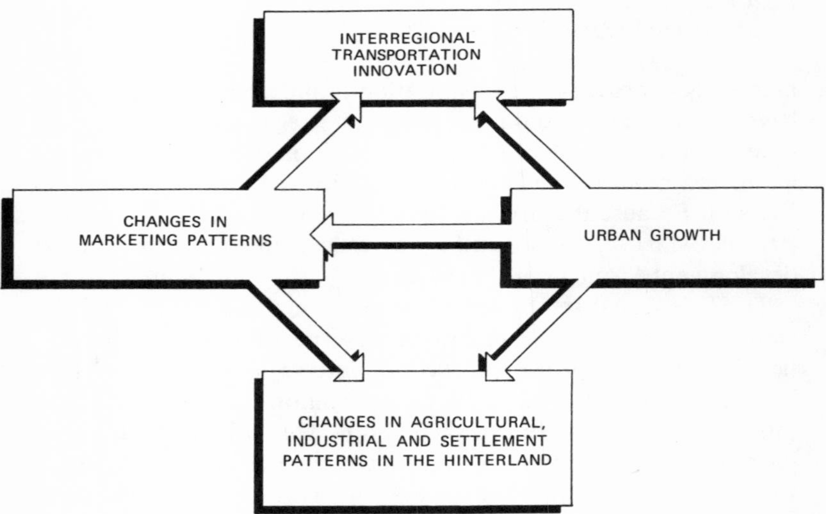

Figure 3. The Process of Change in Onondaga County, 1840-1860

ship over time between the two and among local, sectional, and national forces. The following three chapters deal with the process of urban and regional development in Onondaga County: Chapter 2 with the early settlement period (roughly 1790 to 1820); Chapter 3 with the canal period (roughly 1820 to 1840); and Chapter 4 with the railroad period (roughly 1840 to 1860). Chapters 5 and 6 examine the effect of urban growth and regional economic changes on the populations of both city and hinterland. Chapter 7 summarizes what has been learned about urban growth and regional development in Onondaga County and places the study in the context of broader questions of regional development.

Notes

1. Recent studies that have examined both settlements and their hinterlands together are Robert R. Dykstra, *The Cattle Towns* (New York: Alfred A. Knopf, 1968); Robert Higgs, "The Growth of Cities in a Midwestern Region, 1870-1900," *Journal of Regional Science,* 9 (1969), 369-375; and Edward K. Muller, "Selective Urban Growth in the Middle Ohio Valley, 1800-1860," *The Geographical Review*, 66 (1976), 178-199. Michael Conzen examined one aspect of this relationship in his *Frontier Farming in an Urban Shadow: The Influence of Madison's Proximity on the Agricultural Development of Blooming Grove, Wisconsin* (Madison: State Historical Society of Wisconsin, 1971). Studies of the commercial impact of large multi-state hinterlands include Robert G. Albion, *The Rise of New York Port, 1815-1860* (New York: Charles Scribner's Sons, 1939); and Julius Rubin, "Urban Growth and Regional Development," in David Gilchrist, ed., *The Growth of the Seaport Cities, 1790-1825,* Eleutherian Mills-Hagley Foundation (Charlottesville: University Press of Virginia, 1967). A recent study that examines the effect of the construction of a new transportation system on a small town is Stuart M. Blumin, *The Urban Threshold: Growth and Change in a Nineteenth Century Community* (Chicago: University of Chicago Press, 1976). Studies of trade and transportation rivalries are found in Julius Rubin, *Canal or Railroad? Imitation and Innovation in the Response to the Erie Canal in Philadelphia, Baltimore, and Boston* (Philadelphia: Transactions of the American Philosophical Society, New Series, Vol. 51, part 7, 1961); and Charles N. Glaab, *Kansas City and the Railroads* (Madison: State Historical Society of Wisconsin, 1962). Turner's early work on the economics of sectionalism can be found in Ray Allen Billington, ed., *Frontier and Section: Selected*

Essays of Frederick Jackson Turner (Englewood Cliffs, N.J.: Prentice-Hall, 1961), pp. 115-153. Douglass North has examined interregional economic relationships more recently in *The Economic Growth of the United States, 1790-1860* (Englewood Cliffs, N.J.: Prentice-Hall, 1961).

2. Eric E. Lampard, "The Evolving System of Cities in the United States: Urbanization and Economic Development," in *Issues in Urban Economics,* Harvey S. Perloff and Lowdon W. Wingo, eds. (Baltimore: Johns Hopkins University Press, 1968), pp. 94-95.

3. Johann Heinrich von Thünen, *The Isolated State,* translated by Carla M. Wartenberg and edited with an introduction by Peter Hall (Oxford and London: Pergamon Press, 1966), p. 7 ff; and Edgar M. Hoover and Joseph L. Fisher, "Research in Regional Economic Growth," Universities-National Bureau Committee on Economic Research, *Problems in the Study of Economic Growth* (New York: National Bureau of Economic Research, 1949), pp. 173-250. For a discussion of Hoover and Fisher's synthesis, see Harvey S. Perloff, et al., *Regions, Resources, and Economic Growth* (Baltimore: Johns Hopkins University Press, 1960), pp. 58-60; and Douglass North, "Location Theory and Regional Economic Growth," *Journal of Political Economy,* 63 (1955), 243-258.

4. Hoover and Fisher, "Research in Regional Economic Growth," pp. 177-179; and North, "Location Theory," p. 257. For a discussion of the effect of regional size on analyses of regional development, see Perloff, et al., *Regions, Resources, and Economic Growth,* p. 61; Otis Dudley Duncan, et al., *Metropolis and Region* (Baltimore: Johns Hopkins University Press, 1960), pp. 29-45; and Duncan, Ray P. Cuzzort and Beverly Duncan, *Statistical Geography: Problems in Analysing Areal Data* (Glencoe, Ill.: The Free Press, 1961), pp. 99-111.

5. For a discussion of the definition of hinterlands and trade areas, see Howard L. Green, "Hinterland Boundaries of New York City and Boston in Southern New England," in Harold M. Mayer and Clyde F. Kohn, eds., *Readings in Urban Geography* (Chicago: University of Chicago Press, 1959), pp. 185-201; and Brian J.L. Berry, *Geography of Market Centers and Retail Distribution* (Englewood Cliffs, N.J.: Prentice-Hall, 1967). Central place theory suggests that settlements have regular, hexagonal hinterlands, yet these are disturbed by variations in topography and traffic routes; see Brian J. L. Berry and Allan Pred, *Central Place Studies: A Bibliography of Theory and Applications* (Philadelphia: Regional Science Research Institute, 1961); and Walter Isard, *Location and Space-Economy* (Cambridge: M.I.T. Press, 1956), pp. 270-275.

6. For a discussion of regional differences in patterns of urbanization, see Higgs, "The Growth of Cities in a Midwestern Region, 1870-1900," p.

369; John R. Borchert, "American Metropolitan Evolution," *The Geographical Review*, 57 (1967), 301-332; and Margaret Walsh, *The Manufacturing Frontier: Pioneer Industry in Antebellum Wisconsin, 1830-1860* (Madison: State Historical Society of Wisconsin, 1972), p. viii.

7. Eric E. Lampard, "The History of Cities in the Economically Advanced Areas," *Economic Development and Cultural Change,* 3 (1955), 82.

CHAPTER 2

Before the Canal: The Development of Frontier Settlements

Settlers began drifting into Onondaga County in the 1780s, shortly after the end of the American Revolution. The first settlers came alone. They were men who lived with the Indians, trading with them and learning how to make salt out of the brine at the salt springs along the shores of Onondaga Lake. But once the Revolution was over, Americans were eager to move into the new territories opening up in the West, and the county's population grew rapidly between 1790 and 1820. The isolated traders and salt makers were soon joined by families who came from the East and wanted to settle and farm the lands surrounding the Indian settlements in what was now Onondaga County. In 1800, slightly over a decade after the first white Americans moved to the area, there was an average of eight people per square mile; by 1810, this had increased nearly fourfold; and by 1820, the county boasted an average of more than fifty people per square mile. Although many of the settlers coming into Onondaga stayed only a few years before moving to even newer frontiers farther west, others spent the rest of their lives in their new Onondaga homes—in the busy villages that were soon strung across the county, in the salt mining camps on the banks of Onondaga Lake, on newly plowed farms near mills or manufactories spread over the countryside, or in dense forests producing ashes for export or barrels and wood needed by the thriving salt works.

The land these new settlers confronted exhibited two distinct types of terrain. It was almost flat in the north, with barely enough slope for drainage, but began to slope in the middle of the county, and became very hilly in the south. Lakes could be found throughout the county from Oneida Lake on the northeastern and Cross Lake on the northwestern boundary to Otisco and Skaneateles Lakes in the southwestern corner. In the center of the county was Onondaga Lake, particularly important because of the salt springs on its southern banks which brought salt water to the surface from deep in the earth. In the north there were three navigable rivers—the Oneida River, the Seneca River, and the Oswego River, all of which met at Three River Point on the boundary between Oswego and Onondaga Counties. Away from the rivers, however, this section of the county also had large areas of swampland, caused by the flatness of the land. The southern half of the county, with its more opulent relief, contained many small, quickly moving streams draining north to Lake Ontario, and in the extreme southern portion of the county draining south to Pennsylvania. Five deep ridges cut through the rough terrain of southern Onondaga, running from north to south and dividing the land into hills and "hollows," as the first American settlers called them. At the beginning of the nineteenth century, the land was heavily forested.[1]

Long before white settlers arrived from the eastern United States, this was the land of the Onondaga Indians and was the center of the Iroquois Confederacy. Visited periodically by French missionaries and traders, the land of the Onondaga was settled twice by groups of French farmers and missionaries. The threat of Indian violence frightened the first colonists into leaving around 1655. The second colony was destroyed by the Indians in 1668, three years after it had been settled. At the time of the American Revolution a century later, the Onondaga sided with the British, attacking frontier settlements and suffering the destruction of their own villages and crops at the hands of a detachment of American forces in 1779. After the war was over, either old antagonisms were forgotten or the strength of the Americans seemed incontrovertible, for in 1786 the Onondaga gave a friendly American trader and interpreter, Ephraim Webster, permission to settle among them. Webster brought a boatload of goods for the Indians from Schenectady and traded them for furs, and after the first year, he lived with the Indians near Onondaga Lake. In the ensuing decades, many other Americans followed him into Onondaga, settling on Indian lands and harvesting the fruit of Indian orchards.[2]

Although the land which became Onondaga County formerly belonged to the Indians, a treaty between the Onondaga and the United States in 1788 turned the land into a part of the Military Tract of New York. As part of the treaty, the Indians ceded to the United States all their land except for a reservation eleven and three-eighths miles long and one-twentieth of a mile wide. This reservation became progressively smaller in subsequent treaties signed in 1793, 1817, and 1822. The federal government intended to give the land in the Military Tract as bounties to veterans of the Revolution, but by the time the county boundaries were drawn in 1794 and the land grants were finally made, most of the former soldiers and officers had lost faith in the government's promises of good land and sold their bounty rights to speculators or prospective settlers. The speculators, in turn, sold smaller pieces of land to settlers in Onondaga County or to migrating farmers in New England and eastern New York. No single speculator or group of speculators bought up the military lands in Onondaga County. While speculative ownership may have retarded settlement on certain parcels of land due to legal complications following multiple sales of the same piece of land, the overall effect of speculation on settlement patterns was negligible.[3]

Not all of the land in Onondaga County was parceled out to veterans when the Military Tract was surveyed. Certain lots were sold to provide money for schools and churches, and "for promoting literature in this State." In addition, the valuable salt springs area surrounding southern Onondaga Lake was held by the state government as the Salt Springs Reservation, and the use of this land was leased to individual salt makers. Finally, the Onondaga Indian Reservation was created in the center of the county, south of the salt springs. Confined by treaty to this reservation, the Onondaga occupied a village called Onondaga Castle. By 1810, however, only 200 Onondagans remained in Onondaga Castle, living in log cabins scattered along a road about a mile in length.

The only other Indian land in the county which was once the center of the Iroquois Confederacy was Lot 97 in the township of Pompey, which was ceded to Hanyer Tewahangaraghkan, an Indian captain in the American Army, as part of the land distribution to veterans. There is no evidence that Tewahangaraghkan ever occupied his land.[4]

Migrating families from the East began to arrive in the 1790s. They came from many directions, but the most common route led from Albany along the Mohawk River to Utica or Fort Stanwix (now Rome). From there, travelers through the wilderness took the water route created by the Western Inland Lock and Navigation Company to Lake Oneida or struck out across deeply rutted roads to the township of Manlius, the eastern gateway to Onondaga County. (Strictly speaking, Manlius was a town, not a township. In New York as in New England, unincorporated political and administrative jurisdictions at the subcounty level are called "towns." Because some confusion between towns and villages may result, these areas will be called townships here and the word "town" reserved for settlements.) Many of the earliest settlers stayed in Manlius, while still others went south to the townships of Pompey, Fabius, or Tully or west to Onondaga, Camillus, or Marcellus, filling in the central and southeastern parts of the county. (See Figure 4.) In the following two decades, additional settlers swarmed into these townships, which soon boasted a number of villages as well as thriving farms. Other migrants founded new settlements in the townships that stretched across the north and those in the southwestern corner of the county. By 1810, the population of the county was over 25,000—four times as large as it had been ten years earlier. The rapid migration into the county slowed down somewhat during the War of 1812 but quickly resumed once the war was over. The Americans had succeeded where the French had failed in establishing permanent settlements in the land of the Onondaga.[5]

Settlement patterns in the growing county were strongly influenced by transportation routes. The major transportation link between Onondaga County and the settlements in the East at this time was the turnpike that entered Onondaga in Manlius and cut westward through the center of the county, eventually reaching Lake

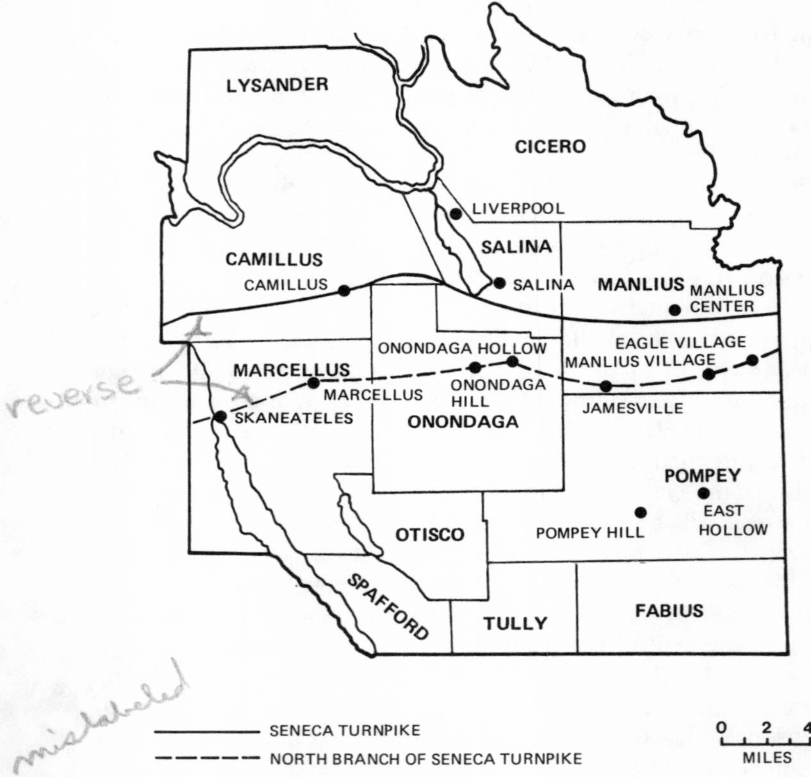

Figure 4. Onondaga County, 1813

Erie in western New York. Called the Genesee Turnpike or the Old State Road in the 1790s and renamed the Seneca Turnpike in the nineteenth century, the former Indian trail quickly became the most important highway to the West for white settlers as well as the principal land route for shipments of salt, wheat, and other county products to eastern markets. With the introduction of regular mail service between Utica and Canandaigua in 1804, scheduled wagons or sleighs crossed the county on the turnpike twice weekly in each direction, weather permitting. Daily service was established in 1808. The most populous townships throughout the decade following 1810 were Manlius, Onondaga, Marcellus, and Pompey—all, except Pompey, located along the turnpike.[6]

Pompey attracted large numbers of settlers from the time the turnpike was little more than an opening through the forest. More of the Revolutionary War grantees took up their land in Pompey than in any other Onondaga township. Yankee immigrants from the declining hill country of New England were also attracted to the hills of Pompey, and they purchased land in the township from grantees who had no wish to live in Onondaga County. Moreover, the early presence of churches, schools, and stores made Pompey seem more settled and civilized to subsequent settlers than the rough settlements at the salt springs or along the turnpike. After 1811, there was the Pompey Academy to educate children. Pompey was well-known both inside and out of Onondaga as a place of wealth and learning, and people from more isolated settlements visited it for legal and medical advice, trading, fashion news, and political discussions. As the township grew, New England farmers spilled over from Pompey into Fabius and Tully and, later, into the townships in the north and southwest of the county.[7]

Outside of Pompey and the other southern townships, Onondaga County was settled by a broader mixture of Yankee and Yorker families. Although many New Englanders settled in the townships crossed by the turnpike, there was a greater variety in the population in these areas, and the communities they helped to establish along the turnpike were not as reminiscent of New England villages as those in the southern part of the county. For example, Manlius attracted many people from eastern New York including Dutch and German settlers from the Mohawk River area and some immigrants from Germany. German and Irish immigrants were also drawn to Salina, where the salt springs provided work for single men with strong backs but no capital for purchasing land of their own.[8]

Although most townships, outside of Salina, were settled largely by farmers and individuals who provided services to the farmers, the county did not have a stable agricultural population. In Onondaga as in other frontier areas, there was a great deal of mobility within as well as into and out of the county during the early years of settlement. Settlers came to Onondaga, stayed for a while, and then moved on. Many bought and sold ever better parcels of land in

Onondaga or neighboring counties, while others moved west in hopes of finding more propitious economic circumstances or to be closer to friends or relatives. The persistence rate, or the proportion of those still remaining in a township after a certain number of years, was low, even for those who were landowners. For example, of the 203 men of the town of Camillus who were electors in 1807 (and thus either landholders or tenants), only 41 percent were still present as taxpaying landowners in 1825. Even the churches, laboring under financial straits because of members' frequent moves, acknowledged the problem. The Onondagans who organized the First Presbyterian Church in Marcellus on January 27, 1807, all signed a pledge to support the church as long as "we shall continue to live at no greater distance from the meeting house in said society than we now do, or at greater distance, if the same shall not be more than three miles and a half."[9]

Despite their geographical mobility, residents of early Onondaga County were not necessarily isolated from their families or their past, as Alexis de Tocqueville suggested was typical of frontier residents in the early nineteenth century. Many native-born Onondagans retained relationships that reached back to eastern communities and were perpetuated in the new settlements established in Onondaga County. These kinship and friendship networks assisted migrants in numerous ways before, during, and after migration. For example, many settlers originally came to Onondaga to join former neighbors or relatives already living in the area and familiar with the country. Typical of this pattern of family migration is the experience of Asa Eastwood who grew up near the Hudson River in New York City and moved to Onondaga County in 1817. His brother John Eastwood preceded him to central New York in 1812 when he had purchased 100 acres of "wild land" on Oneida Lake in Madison County. Five years later, John Eastwood was living on his western land. When Asa Eastwood moved west, he not coincidentally bought land on the other side of Oneida Lake in Onondaga County—within five miles of his brother. He immediately opened a store which he ran for several years near his brother's home in Madison County, and the two men remained close neighbors until John Eastwood died in 1842. Nor were they the only members of their family in the West. Relatives of Asa Eastwood's wife joined the Eastwoods in 1822, living with the family and working the farm on shares for several years while Eastwood traveled between Onondaga County and New York City.[10]

This pattern of serial migration within kinship and friendship networks was repeated over and over in Onondaga County. For example, John Meeker, an early entrepreneur in Onondaga County who moved west from Middlefield, Massachusetts, in the first decade of the nineteenth century, established a number of the young sons of his former neighbors as managers of his string of general stores in the Onondaga villages of Manlius, Camillus, Onondaga Hollow, and Skaneateles. These men retained close personal and business connections with each other and with their families in Massachusetts, making Onondaga County, in effect, a social and, as we shall see later, commercial extension of Middlefield in the early nineteenth century.[11]

In addition to the serial migration of extended families and friends to the new settlements in the West, many other families traveled together to their new homes as in the case of the Keeney Valley settlers. Simon Keeney came to Onondaga County from Connecticut in 1794 to clear his land and construct a cabin. He then returned to East Hartford and the next year, he and four other men, brothers and brothers-in-law, sold their land and moved to the Keeney Valley in southern Onondaga with their families (twenty-eight people in all). In time, the families moved from Keeney's cabin to other parts of the valley, and in later years their satisfaction with the area led others from Connecticut to move to Onondaga County. Clearly, migration to the frontier did not involve cutting family ties for these people—nor for the many other families who migrated as a group.[12]

As the farm population in Onondaga County grew, so did the town population. By 1813, there were already thirteen villages in Onondaga important enough to be mentioned in Horatio Gates Spafford's *Gazetteer of the State of New York.* These ranged from the small settlement of Manlius Center, with slightly more than 100 residents, to the villages of Salina and Manlius Village, each with

500 residents. In addition to these villages, a number of hamlets containing less than 100 people were scattered throughout the county.[13] (See Figure 4.)

The location of villages in Onondaga County at this time was determined by one of three factors: interregional transportation routes, access to natural resources, and centrality in a heavily populated agricultural area. By far the largest number of villages were established along the Seneca Turnpike, the former Indian trail which had long been the major land route across the state. It was the principal stage and mail route as well, and travelers and settlers moving westward were an important source of customers for village merchants and village produce. Seven of the thirteen Onondaga villages were located on this important road (one of them, Onondaga Hollow, on the site of a former Indian village, Gis-twe-ah'-na).

In addition to the transportation-oriented towns, three other villages were well situated to exploit the mineral resources of the region and functioned primarily as mining settlements. In this category were the salt springs villages of Salina and Liverpool and the settlement of Gypsumburg (later Camillus) which was founded to mine the newly discovered gypsum in the township of Camillus. The villages of Camillus and Liverpool had transportation advantages as well. Camillus was located on the North Branch of the Seneca Turnpike, built in 1806, and on the highest navigable point of Nine Mile Creek, a waterway that flowed into Onondaga Lake and connected with the water route to the Hudson. Liverpool was also situated on the lake and was considered the best location in the salt springs area for shipping salt.

A third factor in the location of frontier villages was social and commercial centrality for the surrounding agricultural area. The only part of the county with a sufficient agricultural population to support an agricultural trading village off the interregional transportation routes was the eastern portion of the townships of Pompey and Manlius. Here the villages of Pompey Hill, East Hollow, and Manlius Center provided for the needs of their hinterlands.[14]

There was already a great variety in rural village settlement patterns within the Onondaga townships. Salina township, dominated by the salt mining villages of Salina and Liverpool, was clearly the least rural of the townships. An estimated 47 percent of the township's population lived in villages in 1813. In Manlius, where two major turnpikes intersected, approximately 28 percent of the residents lived in these larger villages. The other townships in the county were considerably more rural than these two and had sharply decreasing proportions of their populations in villages. The townships settled last were those farthest from the turnpike on the northern and southern edges of the county (Cicero, Lysander, Spafford, Otisco, Fabius, and Tully) and had no villages at all with more than 100 residents in 1813.[15]

The fact that two townships out of twelve in Onondaga County had 47 and 28 percent of their population in villages so soon after the initial settlement of the area suggests that this was not a region of subsistence agriculture from which local trading villages would only gradually emerge. Moreover, neither township was dominated by a single settlement, suggesting that the growth of towns or villages was a natural part of the settlement process in this area rather than an isolated stimulus or response to it. Most important, since these settlements were most frequently located according to the route of the major interregional transportation system or the potential rewards of extractive industries, the village population level of these townships is evidence of the early integration of Onondaga County in the national economy.

By the time the middle section of the Erie Canal was opened in 1820, roughly thirty years after the first settlers cut their way through the wilderness, Onondaga County had a diversified economy that boasted agriculture, processing and manufacturing industries, and mining or extractive industries. These activities did not suddenly surface after the population reached a specific size or density; rather, they were begun by the original settlers and expanded gradually with the growing population. Grist milling and saw milling, the most basic and necessary forms of industrial activity on the frontier, were established in Onondaga County in the 1790s by the first settlers in the area—some of whom came with the express intention of milling rather than farming. The grist mills were essential if the newcomers were to have wheat bread as an alternative to the far less attractive home-ground cornbread. Most of the grist mills were custom mills, operated by a single proprietor who ground wheat in exchange for a portion of the flour. Some of the larger mills, however, purchased grain from the farmer, ground it, and sold it elsewhere. Between 1810 and 1820, the number of grist mills in the county increased from approximately thirty-eight to fifty-nine, indicating the growing productivity of local agriculture and its increasing need for processing mills.[16]

Saw mills were also essential to the new settler, whose first task was to clear his land of trees and build a home and farm buildings. The saw mill provided one means of turning excess timber into building material and also into a marketable product. Where there was an absence of good mill sites, as in the township of Cicero, clearing the land was unprofitable and proceeded slowly. The first saw mill was built in Manlius in 1792 by Asa Danforth, who transported the gearings for it from Utica. By 1810, there were at least as many saw mills as grist mills in Onondaga, and probably more, and in the following decade the number of saw mills rose markedly because of the growing demand for lumber by the expanding population. In 1820, there were ninety-nine saw mills operating in the county—nearly one saw mill for every 400 residents.[17]

Other processing industries found in pre-canal Onondaga include distilleries, breweries, tanneries, and asheries. The asheries produced potash for export from the ashes of forest products that could not be turned into lumber. The combined value of the lumber and the ashes from unsettled frontier land was such that landowners frequently contracted with a transient woodsman to clear the land in exchange for the wood he was able to remove and sell or convert to ashes. Once the land was partially cleared, the agricultural settler and his family moved to Onondaga. The ubiquitous frontier distillery provided the farmer with an alternative means of marketing his grain. Rye, corn, barley, and hops were used in making whiskey, which was sold for 25 cents a gallon or for one bushel of corn. Samuel Litherland, whose brewery on Skaneateles Creek was visited by the census taker in 1820, reported that he manufactured 400 to 500 barrels of "brew" each winter which he then marketed throughout Onondaga and the surrounding counties and even in some parts of Canada. Apparently there were some dangers involved in processing the "devil's brew," however, for one luckless frontier distiller, a more temperate local historian dutifully recorded, boiled himself to death in his own mash tub.[18]

Industry on the frontier was not confined to serving the agricultural population. An iron maker, Nicholas Mickles, established a foundry in the township of Onondaga in the early 1790s. During the War of 1812, Mickles had a government contract to produce a large quantity of ammunition for the army and navy in western New York. In peacetime, he also made stoves, pans, kettles, and skillets which he sold to storekeepers in Salina. The goods produced in Mickles's foundry were both heavier and more expensive than similar articles available to settlers, and storekeepers complained that sales came slowly when they came at all. Yet despite slow local sales of household items, Mickles did well producing kettles for salt boiling, stoves, and machinery. In 1820, a year of poor markets and cash shortages in Onondaga following the Panic of 1819, his foundry consumed 320 tons of ore and manufactured articles with a market value of $18,260. At this time he employed eighteen men, one woman, and two children.[19]

In addition to the iron works, Onondaga industries included fulling mills and carding machines for the processing of home-manufactured cloth, cotton and woolen factories, several furniture manufactories, a paper mill, hat factories, and a factory which manufactured wooden pails, bowls, and peck and half-bushel measures. One factory in the county in 1820 employed two men, two women, and four children in the manufacture of tubs, pails, and cooper's ware—the hoop and sheet iron, iron wire, paints, and timber parts used in making barrels. Another small Onondaga firm produced the carding and spinning machines so essential in areas of household manufacture of cloth. There was also a notable furniture industry in the county before the construction of the Erie Canal, for DeWitt Clinton, traveling through Onondaga County in 1810, mentions the "handsome furniture" of curled maple, wild cherry, and black walnut produced there. By 1820, there were six furniture manufactories employing a total of fourteen people.[20]

Prior to the improvement of interregional transportation connections resulting from the construction of the Erie Canal, industrial activities were located in rural areas, independent of residential or commercial centers, and in small towns or hamlets. Industrial centers were not inevitably population centers as well, for there were a number of rural industrial enclaves located on good water power sites several miles from any town or village settlement. One example of this is "Factory Gulf," an industrial center in Spafford. Its location on the Hamilton and Skaneateles Turnpike provided access to the markets it lacked because it had no resident population. Many other industrial complexes were located near but not in large settlements. Within two miles of Manlius Village, for example, there were two fulling mills and two carding machines, five saw mills, four grist mills, an oil mill, two nail factories, and a cotton and woolen factory. Similarly, several miles north of the town of Skaneateles there was another industrial complex with four grist and four saw mills, three fulling mills, three carding machines, and two trip hammers.[21]

Since Onondaga villages frequently expanded after the first mills in the county were built, it is reasonable to ask why towns did not grow up around existing industrial centers or on new industrial sites. Simply put, industrial centers and population centers had different locational needs at this time. Most important in the location of good industrial sites was access to water power; access to the industry's market was of secondary importance. For customers of local processing industries, access to a rural mill was perhaps no more difficult than access to a town on an interregional transportation route. Within the region, transportation away from the turnpikes was difficult whether to towns or to mills and factories. In marked contrast to industrial sites, the success of settlements, as explained earlier, was dependent upon the location of either interregional transportation systems or extractive industries. As the population grew, social and commercial centrality for the surrounding rural hinterland became an increasingly important factor in the location of settlements. If navigable, the fast-moving streams that provided water power for industrial uses were most important to the towns and villages as additional transportation routes. For example, Nine Mile Creek, Limestone Creek, and Butternut Creek were declared public highways by the state legislature in 1801 and penalties were set for obstructing these streams. At times, however, the transportation needs of settlers and the water power needs of industry were directly antithetical as when Jonas C.

Baldwin built a dam and a mill on the Seneca River. Because his construction interfered with travel on the river, he was forced to build a small canal around the dam in 1809 for those using the river as a highway.[22]

Industries located in or near settlements were frequently owned and operated by the same people who ran the local commercial establishments. In 1817 when Asa Eastwood and his partner purchased a house in which to operate their general store, they also built an ashery and a distillery to process their customers' wood ashes and grain. This way they could market ashes and grain for local farmers who would in turn use the money they received to purchase goods from Eastwood and Hall. John Meeker, entrepreneur *par excellence* in Onondaga County, operated both stores and factories throughout the county, and Azariah Smith, one of Meeker's more successful protégés, ran both a cotton factory and a general store in Manlius.

Because the residential decisions of owner-operators were influenced by personal relationships as well as by economic factors, industrial location decisions were also made according to a variety of criteria. These included access to power sites and the contemporary real estate and retail markets, but they were not confined to impersonal economic considerations. Eastwood, as we have seen, wanted to live near his brother, and Smith originally came to Manlius to work for his former fellow townsman from Middlefield, Massachusetts, John Meeker. The importance of social factors in making economic decisions during the settlement of a frontier area was not unique to Onondaga County; for example, Michael Conzen also found this to be the case in his examination of the township of Blooming Grove in Wisconsin.[23]

Although many industries were located in rural areas, they were not scattered at random throughout the county, but were generally located in the rural sections of the most populous townships. The high association between the number of grist mills in a township and the population of that township in 1810 (r = .855) declined only slightly in 1820 (r = .753). While the correlation between the number of saw mills and a town's population in 1810 was considerably lower (r = .433), with the large increase in the number of saw mills in the county between 1810 and 1820, generally in the fastest growing townships, this correlation rose to .938 in 1820. The strength of the correlation suggests that the service areas of locally manufactured and processed goods were narrow and that water power sites close to heavily populated areas were exploited most fully.[24]

Onondaga industries produced goods largely for the resident population and for travelers and settlers passing through the county on their way west. The firms were small—most employed only one or two people—and the initial investment required in most frontier industries was low. An ashery, for example, could be equipped for $20. A few of the more specialized industries such as the paper mill, iron making, and wooden measures and tableware manufacturing probably had a somewhat broader marketing range; however, these goods were still distributed directly by the manufacturer on site and through general stores in the nearby villages. There is no evidence of an interregional marketing system for county-produced items except in salt, agricultural produce, and distilled liquor.[25]

Far more important than local processing and consumption industries to Onondaga's integration in the national economy were the extractive industries exploiting the county's abundant mineral resources. The most important export was salt, obtained from the brine at the salt springs which extended in a half-moon around the southern end of Onondaga Lake. Like the Indians, the early settlers produced enough salt for their own use, but they were also aware of the commercial potential of the salt springs. The demand for salt was particularly great in the West, and the Onondaga salt springs were the only known western source of salt. By 1810, salt works with national market connections had been established in Onondaga at Salina (hence the name); Liverpool, three miles north of Salina on the lake; and Geddes, to the west of Salina. Salt making dominated the economies of these villages, which by 1810 were shipping salt to New York City and the eastern markets, west to Pennsylvania, Ohio, and the Michigan Territory, and also supplying the whole of Upper Canada and a share of Lower Canada. Christian Schultz, a traveler who visited the salt works in 1807, reported that Salina and Liverpool together produced 2,400 bushels of salt a day, using a total of 444 kettles day and night for boiling the saline water from which the salt was obtained. Three years later, DeWitt Clinton observed 807 kettles in use at the salt works.[26]

A second mineral resource in Onondaga County was gypsum, first discovered in the United States in 1792 in the township of Camillus. In 1809, the land where the gypsum was found was purchased by a corporation which began to mine it commercially, and the next year 100 tons of Camillus gypsum were sold. Further gypsum deposits were discovered in Manlius in 1811. In addition to its value as an export, gypsum was used locally on agricultural land to improve productivity.[27]

Both the salt and gypsum industries stimulated other economic activity in the county. The production of gypsum required mills to grind the mineral before it could be sold. Providing firewood to the salt works became the basis for another local industry. Wood was essential for the continual fires that evaporated the salt water, and large areas of the county were systematically denuded to feed the fires of the salt boilers. DeWitt Clinton, while voicing general approval of what he saw in Onondaga County in 1810, was alarmed by the shortsighted way in which wood was procured for the salt works: "The wood on the [salt springs] reservation is cut without any regard to economy, and no adequate measures have been taken to prevent this evil, or to provide for the growth of young timber."[28]

The cooperage industry was a third economic activity stimulated by the mining industry. The salt makers' need for barrels for transporting salt was met by coopers in the forested townships surrounding Salina. Even potash, produced when settlers cleared their land of timber, was transported in barrels in the early years of the county. At one point, a local historian suggests, the cooperage industry "nearly equalled in extent the business that gave it existence." The importance of the market for cooperage encouraged one Onondaga resident to invent machinery for manufacturing parts for barrels. He predicted that because of the great demand for barrels, he would receive a 40 percent profit from the sale of his machinery.[29]

By 1820, as the scope and importance of pre-canal industries indicate, Onondaga County had a mixed agricultural and industrial economy. This was reflected in the composition of the labor force as well. Compared to the older eastern counties of Albany and Schenectady, Onondaga had proportionately more agriculturists and fewer workers employed in commerce or manufacturing. However, the proportion of the adult white male population engaged in agriculture in Onondaga was considerably less than in the western state of Ohio. While two-thirds of the white male labor force in Onondaga County was engaged in agricultural occupations, an additional 16 percent were employed in manufacturing and one percent in commercial occupations. The most heavily agricultural townships, defined in terms of male employment in agriculture, were the southeastern sections of the county, including the townships of Pompey, Tully, Fabius, Spafford, and, to a lesser extent, Camillus and Otisco. With the exception of Camillus, these townships were settled early in the development of the county, lacked mineral resources, and were located away from the major interregional transportation routes. In contrast, Salina had as high a proportion of the labor force in manufacturing as other townships had in agriculture because of the dominance of the salt springs villages in the township.[30]

If Onondaga was underrepresented in any employment sector of the economy, it was in commerce not industry. Although there was commercial activity, those engaged in commerce were usually also involved in agriculture or industry as well. In no sense was the county commercially isolated, for there was constant business contact between residents of Onondaga County and commercial firms in the eastern United States and a considerable interregional trade in effect as early as 1810. Agricultural produce and mineral resources were exported and grocery items such as sugar and spices were imported. Onondagans used two distinct types of markets at this time: agricultural markets and salt markets. Farmers or local shopkeepers generally marketed agricultural products in the cities of eastern New York. In contrast, salt was marketed in all directions from the salt springs at the base of Onondaga Lake. These were used almost entirely for the salt trade, although agricultural products were occasionally shipped east with the salt. Eastern merchants with national commercial interests, who frequently employed only an agent to represent them in Onondaga County, arranged for the transportation of these shipments.

A number of different routes extended the market for Onondaga salt over almost half a continent. (1) Salt was shipped east to New York City. (2) The lands immediately to the south of Onondaga were supplied by wagons that brought the salt to the "salt landing" in Homer, a village in neighboring Cortland County on the navigable Chenango River. From there the salt could be taken by water into southern New York and northern Pennsylvania. (3) Another route to the south was to ship the salt west by the Seneca River to Cayuga and Seneca Lakes and, after a short portage over the divide, by the Susquehanna River system to the Chesapeake Bay or by the Allegheny River to the Ohio River. (4) North of the salt works, the salt was sent by boat down the Oswego River to Lake Ontario and from there down the St. Lawrence River to Montreal. (5) More frequently, however, the salt-laden boats turned west toward Lake Erie, portaging the distance overland between the lakes. (6) Salt also reached Lake Erie by land, crossing western New York in wagons drawn by six to eight teams of horses. From Lake Erie, the salt was conveyed in various combinations of land and water transport to Pittsburgh, Cleveland, Detroit, and even as far south as Cincinnati.[31]

In short, there was an extensive trading network for the sale of Onondaga salt prior to the construction of the Erie Canal. This was reflected in the increased production of salt in the county. Annual production rose from 25,474 bushels in 1797, the year that the state formally assumed control of the salt springs reservation, to 458,329 bushels in 1820 when the first section of the canal was opened to traffic. The average annual increase between 1810 and 1820 was 30,004 bushels. While transportation from the salt springs to the dispersed markets was somewhat slow, it was not impossible. The most common mode of travel was by water and the most difficult portions of the trip were the portages. Yet even here the scale of the traffic led to certain efficiencies. At the height of the trade between the Onondaga salt works and Pittsburgh, for example, there were a hundred teams of oxen continually at work carting salt between the port at Erie, Pennsylvania, and Waterford, the river town on the inland water route to Pittsburgh. It is entirely conceivable that even without the canal, these trading networks would eventually have been expanded to include products other than salt.[32]

In contrast to the salt markets, the commercial and agricultural markets for Onondaga County were all in the East where interregional wholesale marketing facilities already existed. The major wholesale markets were Utica, Albany, New York City, and Montreal. Many county storekeepers sold produce in Albany and purchased manufactured and imported goods in New York City, while farmers sold their own produce in Utica, Albany, or Montreal. Local merchants usually made two buying trips to the East every year—one in November and one in May or June. Often they brought potash, wheat, and oats to the markets and then loaded the same wagons with drugs, hardware, and groceries (goods not produced or manufactured in Onondaga) for the return trip. As the traffic between the Hudson River and western New York increased after the War of 1812, teamsters also extended their services. This enabled Onondaga residents to hire drivers with wagons to bring their produce to market. In time, certain local merchants—often the agents for larger Eastern-based merchants—no longer made buying trips themselves but merely shipped salt and flour east and received wholesale goods delivered by teamsters in return.

Land transportation to the East was easier when the ground froze in the winter and farmers could use sleighs to carry their goods to market. Although shopkeepers tended to ship their goods from the East at any time of the year, farmers in Onondaga waited for sleighing weather. This was in part because the frozen ground made it easier to transport heavy loads and in part because of the rhythms of farm life, which gave the farmer time to leave his farm in the winter.[33]

In addition to transporting goods by land, Onondaga residents could move goods to and from Albany by water. The Western Inland Lock and Navigation Company, chartered by the state legislature in 1792, created a water route from Lake Oneida on the northeastern border of Onondaga County to the Mohawk River, opening a direct water route between Onondaga County and the Hudson River. Many boats carrying shipments from Albany and Schenectady continued from Lake Oneida down the Oswego River to reach Lake Ontario and the Canadian and western markets; a steamboat was built for this trade on Lake Oneida in 1817. However, the water route between Onondaga and Albany was not used as much as its promoters had expected, for they were unable to avoid a portage from the Mohawk River to the Hudson River or periods of low water in winding rivers—both of which slowed transportation and raised transportation costs.[34]

Evidence of the commercial, rather than subsistence, orientation of the economy can be seen in the importance of capital to Onondagans in the years before the construction of the Erie Canal. Although county residents often bartered agricultural produce for imported goods at the local general store, these items were then resold to other customers or taken to the eastern markets for sale. Moreover, capital was essential to the frontier merchant, who did not operate in a barter economy, and to the farmer who needed capital for mortgage payments. At times very large sums of money were invested in goods for Onondaga stores. John Meeker, for example, was supposedly advanced $70,000 in goods for his stores in 1808; business was apparently very good, for the following spring he purchased an additional $40,000 worth of goods. This was not merely for one establishment: Meeker had a chain of seven stores at the time and divided the inventory between them, keeping each store continually stocked with about $8,000 in goods. The need of the residents of Onondaga for capital was further underscored by their enthusiastic response in 1809 to the repeal of Jefferson's Embargo, which had caused a capital scarcity in the county. Three thousand people, both Federalists and Republicans, gathered in Manlius Village to celebrate repeal with toasts, bands, cannon, and liberty poles.

Changes in the national economy had a direct effect on the economy of Onondaga County. The scarcity of cash needed to pay salt duties at the time of the embargo was probably responsible for the decline in the population of Salina between 1810 and 1814. Similarly, the impact in Onondaga of the Panic of 1819, caused in part by a sharp decline in the European demand for American foodstuffs and a constriction in the amount of capital in circulation in the United States, is further evidence of the close ties between Onondaga County and the national economy and the importance of cash to the local economy. County manufacturers were almost unanimous in their complaints in 1820 that business had slowed down and that cash sales had at times almost disappeared in the aftermath of the panic.[35]

Instead of discouraging commercial activity, the final effect of the capital scarcity on the frontier was to strengthen commercial ties with the east and to encourage financial dependence upon families. Capital was normally obtained in Onondaga from eastern banks, eastern relatives, or sales of salt and produce. With the nearest bank in Utica, the lack of local banking facilities was keenly felt, and in 1814 petitions were presented to the New York State Assembly for the establishment of a bank in Onondaga County. Although the petitions were approved, no bank was established in the county until 1830. In the interim, banking functions were often performed by local merchants, who held the largest local supplies of capital. In addition, funds flowed between the immigrants' old homes and their new businesses. A number of frontier businessmen were initially financed by relatives and friends in the East. It is likely, moreover, that capital moved both ways, for as Onondaga businesses became more successful, profits could be sent back East and invested in personal loans.[36]

Accessibility to finance capital in the East often meant the difference between successful and unsuccessful commercial operations. Azariah Smith, an immigrant to Onondaga County from Middlefield, Massachusetts, clerked for John Meeker for three years before opening his own store with capital from his savings and from his parents. Smith chose to go into partnership with Calvin Smith, a Middlefield cousin who was also one of Meeker's clerks, rather than with his own brother, because the combined capital available to the cousins, drawing upon money from two sets of parents for purchasing stock for the store, would be greater than that of the brothers. The beneficial effects of kinship networks did not accrue only to frontier migrants. In Smith's case, for example, profits from his Manlius store were in time channeled back to Massachusetts and invested in loans to people in the parent community.[37]

In addition to its financial ties with the East, Onondaga County by 1820 also had extensive transportation connections with eastern New York and southern New England. The original settlers had traveled on roads that were little more than forest paths, many of them Indian trails, but with the settlement of the county in the 1790s, the construction of major interregional turnpikes across the state began. A number of these roads, such as the Seneca Turnpike, the Third Great Western Turnpike, and the North Branch of the Seneca Turnpike, went through Onondaga County as did many shorter regional roads which connected western villages. Publicly constructed turnpikes were financed by lotteries and by taxing property owners along the route of the new road, and privately owned and managed roads were financed by selling stock in the turnpike company. Onondaga County benefited in two ways from the expansion of the turnpike system. The construction of the roads attracted new settlers to the area through improved transportation and also provided jobs and construction contracts to county residents, who often received stock in the highway as compensation for their efforts.[38]

The turnpikes and highways built prior to 1810 generally ran on a lateral east-west axis, indicating the strong orientation of the section to the East in the initial period of settlement. These highways were built to move western products to markets in the East and bring settlers and trading goods to the West. However, several roads built between 1804 and 1808 were exceptions to the general pattern of east-west lateral roads. These all originated in central New York and led to the salt springs in the center of the county.

Between 1810 and 1820, patterns of highway construction changed markedly with most new roads constructed on a north-south axis. This signaled the beginning of a multi-county regional orientation in central New York, as opposed to the previously dominant east-west orientation. Many new roads originated in southern New York and terminated in those Onondaga villages located on one or more of the east-west highways or turnpikes. Others were built to provide access to Onondaga's mineral resources, such as the Salt and Gypsum Turnpike, running from de Ruyter, in neighboring Madison County, to Manlius Village. Whatever the original purpose of the roads, the effect of their construction was to improve backcountry transportation and communication and ultimately to stimulate intercounty regional trade. This process was interrupted by the introduction of a new element into the transportation system: the Erie Canal. By 1819, its influence could already be seen in the proposal for the Corinth and Tully Turnpike, a highway that was planned to run from the Hamilton and Skaneateles Turnpike in Tully to the Erie Canal at Corinth, the newborn canal settlement that would soon be renamed Syracuse.[39]

The early years of Onondaga County, before the construction of the Erie Canal, illustrate the importance of interregional economic and transportation connections in the growth of an undeveloped region in this period. The townships that lay along the path of the turnpike grew more quickly and were larger by 1820 than townships located off the turnpike—despite the fact that land on the turnpike was considerably more expensive than land even a mile away. The first villages in the county also grew up along the Seneca Turnpike. In part, this reflected the importance of trade to the residents of the county, for the turnpike provided access to eastern markets and, increasingly, a steady stream of temporary customers migrating to western lands. In addition, the turnpike was a valuable link with the East for the frontier settler, whose social and family ties provided economic as well as social support during and after migration to Onondaga. Neither isolated nor, because of transportation difficulties and the length of time required to travel East, totally dependent upon outside manufacturing and processing, the county prior to 1820 was still within the effective trading hinterland of a number of New York cities at various stages in the distribution chain. More important, Onondaga County was a functioning part of the national economy.[40]

Notes

1. Willis Gaylord, "Agriculture of Onondaga County," *Transactions of the New York State Agricultural Society*, II (Albany: E. Mach, 1843), 174-178; and W. W. Clayton, *History of Onondaga County, New York* (Syracuse: Mason & Co., 1878), pp. 55, 67.

2. Horatio Gates Spafford, *A Gazetteer of the State of New York* (Albany: H. C. Southwick, 1813), pp. 90, 261; Lewis Henry Morgan, *League of the Ho-De-No Sau-Nee or Iroquois*, II (New York: Dodd, Mead & Co., 1901; reprinted, New Haven: Human Relations Area Files, 1954), pp. 86-88; Dwight H. Bruce, *Onondaga's Centennial: Gleanings of a Century*, II (n.p. [Boston]; Boston History Company, 1896), pp. 247-248;

and Dwight H. Bruce, *Memorial History of Syracuse* (Syracuse: H. P. Smith & Co., 1891), p. 382. Settlers in Pompey (later LaFayette) were able to take over a profitable orchard which had previously belonged to the Indians. See Joshua V. H. Clark, *Onondaga; or Reminiscences of Earlier and Later Times*, II (Syracuse: Stoddard and Babcock, 1849), p. 283.

3. When Onondaga County was created in 1794, it included parts of what are today Seneca, Cayuga, Oswego, Cortland, and Tompkins counties. Its boundaries were changed in 1799, 1808, and 1816. With the removal of Oswego County in 1816 it attained its present size. The following account for the pre-1820 period deals only with the area that eventually remained Onondaga County. See Clark, *Onondaga*, I (1849), pp. 283, 337-348; Bruce, *Memorial History*, pp. 48-53; and J. H. French, *Gazetteer of the State of New York*...(Syracuse: R. P. Smith, 1860), pp. 472-478.

4. Paul W. Gates, *The Farmer's Age, 1815-1860* (New York: Holt, Rinehart and Winston, 1960), pp. 29-30; Clark, *Onondaga*, II, pp. 7-44, 247-248; Bruce, *Memorial History*, p. 382; Bruce, *Onondaga's Centennial*, I, pp. 9, 595; and Spafford, *Gazetteer* (1813), p. 261. Spafford, writing in 1813, showed an unusual interest in the history and contemporary condition of the Onondaga Indians.

5. William H. Webster and Melville R. Webster, *History and Genealogy of the Governor John Webster Family of Connecticut* (Rochester: E. R. Andrews Printing Company, 1915), pp. 389-392. If we assume that the intercensal population increase was the same each year, the yearly increase between 1800 and 1810 was 1,906 people. Between 1810 and 1814, the yearly increase declined to 1,131, but this rose to 1,908 per year between 1814 and 1820. Since the base population was constantly rising, the rate of increase was lower between 1814 and 1820 than it was between 1800 and 1810, despite the fact that in absolute numbers the yearly increase was slightly higher. Population data, unless otherwise noted, are taken from the federal and state censuses listed in the bibliography. For comments on migration during the War of 1812, see also Bruce, *Onondaga's Centennial*, I, p. 218.

6. Morgan, *League of the Iroquois*, II, pp. 86-88; Bruce, *Memorial History*, p. 46; and Bruce, *Onondaga's Centennial*, I, p. 199.

7. Spafford, *Gazetteer* (1813), p. 275; Clark, *Onondaga*, II, p. 241, 248; and Carroll E. Smith, *Pioneer Times in the Onondaga County* (Syracuse: C. W. Bardeen, 1904), pp. 96, 100.

8. Bruce, *Onondaga's Centennial*, II, p. 953; Clark, *Onondaga*, II, p. 148.

9. This persistence rate, although low, is high for the United States in the nineteenth century. Peter R. Knights, for example, found that only 27.8 percent of the population of Boston in 1830 was still present in 1849 in

The Plain People of Boston: A Study in City Growth (New York: Oxford University Press, 1971), p. 57. The higher persistence rate observed in Onondaga County was undoubtedly influenced by the fact that it applied to landowners rather than the general public. See also George R. Smith, *A History of the First Eighty Years of the First Presbyterian Church of Marcellus, N.Y.* (Canandaigua, N.Y.: Ontario County Times, 1883), p. 13; Bruce, *Onondaga's Centennial*, II, pp. 663-665, 673-677, 692-698, and 731-733.

10. For the tendency of extended families and neighborhoods to migrate as a group, see Lois Kimball Mathews, *The Expansion of New England: The Spread of New England Settlement and Institutions to the Mississippi River, 1620-1865* (New York: Russell and Russell, 1972; originally pub-lished, 1909); and Whitney R. Cross, *The Burned-Over District: The Social and Intellectual History of Enthusiastic Religion in Western New York, 1800-1850* (Ithaca: Cornell University Press, 1950), pp. 5-6. See also the Asa Eastwood Papers, 1804-1872, George Arents Research Library, Syracuse University. The importance of kinship networks in assisting the urban migrant at the time of migration and in the receiving community has been explored for the twentieth century by Eugene Litwak, "Geographical Mobility and Extended Family Cohesion," *American Sociological Review*, 25 (1960), 9-21; Charles Tilly and C. Harold Brown, "On Uprooting, Kinship, and the Auspices of Migration," *International Journal of Comparative Sociology*, 8 (1967), 139-164; and Harvey M. Choldin, "Kinship Networks in the Migration Process," *International Migration Review*, 7 (1973), 163-175. The social and economic importance of kinship networks on the agricultural frontier has yet to be explored, although the evidence in Onondaga County indicates that kinship connections provided valuable support to migrants in the settlement of the county.

11. Edward Church Smith and Phillip Mack Smith, *A History of the Town of Middlefield, Massachusetts* (Menasha, Wis.: The Collegiate Press, 1924); Herbert Barber Howe, "John Meeker, 1767-1840" (typescript, Syracuse Public Library); and Mary Josephine Hasbrouck, "Why Early Settlers Came to Onondaga County" (Paper delivered to the Onondaga Historical Association, March 11, 1938), pp. 16-19.

12. Webster and Webster, *History and Genealogy of the Governor John Webster Family*, pp. 389-392; Bruce, *Onondaga's Centennial*, I, p. 869.

13. The number of residents of these villages can be estimated from the number of houses in each settlement multiplied by 5.4. This number is derived from Spafford's description of Onondaga Hollow in his 1813 *Gazetteer*, p. 261. He reports that the village had 350 people and 65 houses, or an average of 5.4 persons per dwelling. Assuming that village housing conditions were roughly similar throughout the county, we can multiply

the number of houses by 5.4 to calculate the approximate population of each village.

14. Morgan, *League of the Iroquois*, II, pp. 86-88.

15. Estimates of the village population were made by multiplying the number of houses in each village by 5.4 (see note 13). Although residents of the village of Salina were likely to have had smaller families, the salt workers were also more likely to live in dormitory worker housing with a high number of residents per house than were workers in other county villages. If anything, the proportion of Salina residents in the two salt villages is an underestimate. See Spafford, *Gazetteer* (1813), and Christian Schultz, *Travels on an Inland Voyage through the States of New York, Pennsylvania, Virginia, Ohio, Kentucky, and Tennessee, and through the Territories of Indiana, Louisiana, Mississippi and New Orleans; performed in the years 1807 and 1808* (New York: I. Riley, 1810), Letter III, for a description of the villages, and Bruce, *Memorial History*, p. 119, for a description of housing for salt workers. William W. Campbell, *The Life and Writings of DeWitt Clinton* (New York: Baker and Scribner, 1849), pp. 183-185, contains Clinton's observations.

16. The word "industry" is used here as it was used in the nineteenth century—to refer to an economic activity that produces an object with commercial value—and can apply to manufacturing, mining, and processing raw materials. It does not necessarily indicate factory production. Erasmus Carr, "Remarks concerning the early history of the township of Tully, N.Y." (typescript, July 29, 1910, Syracuse Public Library); Clarence H. Danhof, *Change in Agriculture: The Northern United States, 1820-1870* (Cambridge: Harvard University Press, 1969), p. 31; Charles B. Kuhlmann, "Processing Agricultural Products in the Pre-Railway Age," in Harold Williamson, ed., *The Growth of the American Economy* (New York: Prentice-Hall, 1951), p. 161; *United States Census, 1820*; and Edmund Norman Leslie, *Skaneateles: History of its Earliest Settlement and Reminiscences of Later Times* (New York: Andrew H. Kellogg, 1902), pp. 83-84. The figures on the number of grist mills in 1810 are estimates based upon the figures given by Spafford, *Gazetteer* (1813). His figures, however, are both approximate and incomplete. Whenever he was indefinite, the lowest of his estimates was used. For the towns of Onondaga and Pompey, where he neglected to give the number of mills, estimates were made based on the number of mills in demographically similar towns.

17. Estimates of the number of saw mills in 1810 were made in the same way as the estimates of the number of grist mills. Bruce. *Onondaga's Centennial*, I, pp. 185, 453, 843; and Clark, *Onondaga*, II, p. 383.

18. Clark, *Onondaga*, II, p. 234; Lena Putnam Anguish, *History of Fayetteville-Manlius Area* (Manlius, N.Y.: Fayetteville-Manlius Central

School District, 1966), p. 26; Leslie, *Skaneateles*, p. 121; Spafford, *Gazetteer* (1813); and George Knapp Collins, *Spafford, Onondaga County, New York* (n.p.: Dehler Press, 1917), pp. 59-61.

19. For information on Nicholas Mickles and his business, see Joshua V. H. Clarke, *Lights and Lines of Indian Character, and Scenes of Pioneer Life* (Syracuse: E. H. Babcock and Co., 1854), p. 337; and the correspondence from Isaac Northrup to the firm of Dexter and Moseley, Salina, May 26, 1820, Simon Newton Dexter Collection, Department of Manuscripts and University Archives, Cornell University. See also the Digest of Accounts of Manufactures from the 1820 census manuscripts, National Archives; Bruce, *Onondaga's Centennial*, I, pp. 185, 453, 843; and Clark, *Onondaga*, II, p. 383.

20. Digest of Accounts of Manufactures; and Campbell, *Life and Writings of DeWitt Clinton*, pp. 183-185.

21. Spafford, *Gazetter* (1813); Leslie, *Skaneateles*, p. 121; and Collins, *Spafford*, pp. 59-61.

22. Bruce, *Onondaga's Centennial*, I, pp. 217, 743-744.

23. Eastwood papers, Diary, Vol. I, August 14, 1818; letter from Joseph Smith, Manlius, New York, to his parents, Middlefield, Massachusetts, May 5, 1817, reprinted in Albert V. House, Jr., "Two Yankee Traders in New York: Letters on the Financing of Frontier Merchants, 1808-1830," *New England Quarterly,* II (1938), 607-631; and Michael P. Conzen, *Frontier Farming in an Urban Shadow* (Madison: State Historical Society of Wisconsin, 1971), p. 151. See also Melvin L. Greenhut, *Plant Location in Theory and in Practice: The Economics of Space* (Chapel Hill: University of North Carolina Press, 1956), for a discussion of non-economic factors in location decisions.

24. All correlations, unless otherwise noted, are Pearson product moment correlation coefficients.

25. Margaret Walsh stresses the importance of good transportation in the growth of large manufacturing and processing firms on the frontier. See *The Manufacturing Frontier* (Madison: State Historical Society of Wisconsin, 1972), pp. 214-217. Onondaga distilleries produced $63,705.60 worth of whiskey in 1810 alone, according to the *United States Census of Manufacturing, 1810*. See Leslie, *Skaneateles*, p. 121, for a description of the relationship between an industrial center and a village located one mile away.

26. Bruce, *Memorial History*, pp. 90, 382-383; Schultz, *Travels on an Inland Voyage*, Letter III, July 26, 1807; Campbell, *Life and Writings of DeWitt Clinton*, p. 181; and letter from Asa Danforth, Jr., Onondaga County, New York, to Timothy Green, New York City, August 4, 1806, in

the Green Family Papers, George Arents Research Library, Syracuse University.

27. Clark, *Onondaga*, II, pp. 78-79, 235; Horatio Gates Spafford, *A Gazetteer of the State of New York* (Albany: B. D. Packard, 1824), p. 77.

28. Campbell, *Life and Writings of DeWitt Clinton*, p. 181.

29. Clark, *Onondaga*, II, pp. 188, 191; Bruce, *Onondaga's Centennial*, II, p. 952; Leslie, *Skaneateles*, p. 214; and Digest of Accounts of Manufactures (1820), National Archives.

30. U.S. Census Office, *Census for 1820* (Washington: Gales and Seaton, 1821).

31. Marvin A. Rapp, "New York's Trade on the Great Lakes, 1800-1840," *New York History*, 39 (1958), 22-33; letter from Asa Danforth, Jr., Onondaga County, New York, to Timothy Green, New York City, December 19, 1807, Green Family Papers; Mary Carson Darlington, compiler, *Fort Pitt and Letters from the Frontier* (Pittsburgh: J. R. Weldin & Co., 1892), pp. 275-300; Clayton, *History*, opposite p. 141; Alvin Bronson, *An Essay on the Commerce and Transportation of the Vallies of the Great Lakes and Rivers of the North-West* (Oswego, N.Y.: Advertiser and Times Steam Press, 1868), p. 6; Bruce, *Memorial History*, p. 389; William Cooper, *A Guide in the Wilderness or the History of the First Settlements in the Western Counties of New York with useful instructions to Future Settlers* (Dublin: Gilbert & Hodges, 1810), pp. 13-14; John Dobbins, "The Dobbins Papers," *Publications of the Buffalo Historical Society*, 8 (1905), 286-289; and letter to W. A. Bird, January 19, 1866, Oswego, reprinted in William A. Bird, "New York State Early Transportation," *Publications of the Buffalo Historical Society*, 2 (1880), 24-25.

32. *Hunt's Merchants' Magazine*, 34 (1856), 509; Rapp, "New York's Trade," 24-25.

33. Howe, "Meeker" p. 3; Dexter Collection, Department of Manuscripts and University Archives, Cornell University, Ithaca, New York; Bird, "New York State Early Transportation," 24; House, "Two Yankee Traders," 607-31; and George Geddes, *Report on the Agriculture and Industry of the County of Onondaga, State of New York* (Albany: Charles Van Benthuysen, 1860), pp. 26-27.

34. Spafford, *Gazetteer* (1824), p. 114; Clark, *Onondaga*, II, p. 188; Bruce, *Onondaga's Centennial*, I, p. 219; Nathan Miller, *The Enterprise of a Free People: Aspects of Economic Development during the Canal Period, 1792-1838* (Ithaca: Cornell University Press, 1962), pp. 21-22.

35. Letter from Azariah Smith, Manlius Village, New York, to his parents, Middlefield, Massachusetts, March 26, 1808; Smith to his parents, June 17, 1809. The Smith letters were reprinted in House, "Two Yankee

Traders." See also the manuscript schedules of the Digest of Accounts of Manufactures (1820), National Archives. For a discussion of the causes and effects of the Panic of 1819, see Harold M. Somers, "The Performance of the American Economy, 1789-1865," in Williamson, ed., *The Growth of the American Economy.*

36. Letter from Smith to his parents, September 23, 1811; Smith to his parents, March 26, 1808, in House, "Two Yankee Traders"; letter from Asa Danforth, Jr., *Salina*, to Timothy Green, New York City, July 20, 1808, Green Family Papers; *New York Assembly Journal*, 37th Session, 1814, pp. 279, 298; Carol Halpert Schwartz, "Retail Trade Development in New York State in the Nineteenth Century with Special Reference to the Country Store" (Ph.D. dissertation, Columbia University, 1963), pp. 146, 186; and House, "Two Yankee Traders," 607-610.

37. Letter from Smith to his parents, May 11, 1810; see also House, "Two Yankee Traders," 607-631, and Walsh, *Manufacturing Frontier*, p. 11.

38. The sole exception to this road pattern is the highway from Onondaga Hill to Oswego on the west side of Onondaga Lake. This too, however, provided access from yet a different direction to the salt springs. The early nineteenth-century highway network was reconstructed from records, in the papers of the New York State Divisional Engineer's Office, Third District, of legislative commissions appointed to lay out roads along specific routs. A typescript copy of these records is in the Onondaga Historical Association. See Clark, *Onondaga*, II, pp. 187-188, 314; Bruce, *Memorial History*, pp. 41-44; the White Family Papers, Department of Manuscripts and University Archives, Cornell University, Ithaca, New York, which contain statements of highway taxes in arrears for nonpayment; and Bruce, *Onondaga's Centennial*, I, pp. 215-216.

39. The Corinth and Tully Turnpike was probably never built. It was also incorporated in 1827 and re-incorporated in 1831.

40. See DeWitt Clinton's comparison of the price of land on and away from the turnpike in Campbell, *Life and Writings of DeWitt Clinton*, p. 185.

CHAPTER 3

Transportation Innovation and Urban Growth: The Canal

The process of development in Onondaga County was interrupted in 1820 when the middle section of the Erie Canal was opened for traffic. Although the entire length of the canal from Buffalo to Albany would not be finished until 1825, the prospect of its completion was enough to set in motion the forces that were to induce widespread changes in the county. In time the canal permanently altered the turnpike-based transportation patterns that had been built up between Onondaga County and the rest of New York state, and by so doing, it transformed the existing social economy that had been based on that transportation system. The canal network formed by the Erie and Oswego Canals was the first major interregional transportation innovation in Onondaga since the initial settlement of the county. Because of the importance of interregional contacts to the county economy, a change in transportation which shortened the travel time between Onondaga and the eastern settlements was bound to have a major effect on the internal development of the area. By altering the economic relationships between Onondaga County and the East, the canal system also played an important role in establishing a new set of economic relationships within the county as well. The most important result of these changes was the growth of the city of Syracuse. Spawned by the canal and nourished by the steady increase in canal traffic, Syracuse grew from a hamlet on the edge of a swamp to a major interregional transportation center. Secondary but no less important changes in the county derived from the combined impact of the shortened travel time to the East and the evolution of new interregional marketing patterns. These changes included alteration of the existing settlement pattern in the county, shifts in the location and nature of industrial activity, and the reorientation of county agriculture.

A second interregional transportation innovation, the railroad network that was built in Onondaga County between 1836 and 1854, had a weaker effect on the internal development of the county because it tended to reinforce the economic tendencies set in motion by the canal system. Only in the southern part of the county where the canal system did not reach did the railroad have an important influence in altering the development pattern. There its effect was the same as the effect of the canal had been earlier in the rest of the county, suggesting that the impact of the canal system on Onondaga County was due less to its characteristics as a transportation system and more to its function as an interregional connection that shortened the travel time between the local and the national markets. By the time the railroad was built, the hierarchy of settlements in the county had been firmly established. Because Syracuse dominated this hierarchy, the railroad was built to the growing city, further reinforcing Syracuse's position as both an interregional and, increasingly, a regional transportation center.

For all its eventual effect in Onondaga County, the Erie Canal was the result of years of agitation, scheming, and hard work outside the county by New York State canal enthusiasts. Their efforts came to fruition in 1820 when the middle section of the canal was opened to traffic, cutting across Onondaga County and stretching from Montezuma, a village west of the county on the Seneca River, to Utica, a city east of Onondaga on the Mohawk River. Additional sections of the waterway were opened yearly thereafter until 1825 when the entire canal was completed, linking Onondaga County with Lake Erie in the West and the Hudson

River in the East. As early as 1811, the canal's supporters had attempted to interest the federal government in financing its construction by arguing that a New York canal would be national in scope and would offer transportation and commercial advantages to both eastern and western states. However, Washington was not interested in the project. Eventually the proponents of the canal were able to convince the New York State Legislature that the state would benefit economically by having a direct water route from the West. Not only would a canal provide cheap transportation for shipping agricultural products from western New York to eastern markets, but it would also channel to New York City the western goods then being sent to the market in Montreal. Canal advocates also stressed that the canal would facilitate the transportation of salt from the Onondaga salt springs and that the state could profit from the salt duties received as a result of this expansion of the salt market.[1]

Regardless of the arguments presented in Albany for building a canal across the state, the canal's effect on the local level—in this case, within Onondaga County—went far beyond merely providing transportation. Physically, the canal bisected the county, running north of the Seneca Turnpike and parallel to it through the townships of Manlius, Salina, and Camillus. (See Figure 5.) The only village of any size on the direct route of the canal was Manlius Center, which had been the smallest of the county's thirteen villages in 1813. The canal was also routed through a small marginal settlement in a swampy area of the salt springs south of Onondaga Lake. Variously called Milan, Cossitt's Corners, and Corinth, the site received the permanent name of Syracuse in 1820. Although the canal bypassed the salt springs village of Salina, that settlement's salt was so necessary to the success of the waterway that a side cut of one and one-half miles was built to Salina at the time the main canal was built. In 1822, the state authorized the extension of the side cut to Onondaga Lake, thus enabling shippers to transport salt from Liverpool, a salt village on the lake, to the side cut by way of the lake and then to the canal.[2]

The construction of the Oswego Canal in 1828 completed the interregional canal network through Onondaga County. Running south from the port settlement of Oswego on Lake Ontario to Syracuse, the Oswego Canal connected the Erie Canal and Canada and also provided an alternative route for grain shipments from the West. These shipments could be transported around Niagara Falls to Lake Ontario by means of the Welland Canal, built between 1824 and 1829. Cargo-laden canal boats then crossed Lake Ontario to the Oswego Canal and moved south to Syracuse. The major advantage of this route to shippers was that they paid lower canal tolls because they traveled shorter distances on the canals. But regardless of whether western shippers chose the straight path of the Erie Canal or the more roundabout but cheaper route across Lake Ontario to the Oswego Canal, they had to travel through Onondaga County and particularly through Syracuse. Thus the conjunction of these two canals in Syracuse gave a further impetus to the growth of the town by making it a major interregional transportation center.[3]

The canals offered shippers many advantages over the turnpikes. One of the most important immediate advantages of canal transportation was cost. Overland turnpike transportation amounted to between 30 and 70 cents per ton-mile during the first two decades of the nineteenth century. In sharp contrast, canal charges were only 1.68 cents per ton-mile between 1830 and 1850. Moreover, the regularity of canal shipments during the months the canal was in operation (usually from late April or early May to November or December each year) offered farmers and local merchants with county produce to sell important marketing advantages over turnpike transportation. No longer did the weather or the condition of the roads interfere with farmers' attempts to market their produce. Although canal transportation was slow, speed was not important for agricultural produce that was being shipped long distances. If wheat could be shipped considerably more cheaply at the speed of only 1.8 miles per hour by canal, it did not matter that loaded wagons traveling over turnpikes could move at about two miles an hour when the weather was fair and the roads in good condition.[4]

Speed was more crucial for passenger traffic, much of which continued to travel by stage or horseback on the turnpikes where they could go even faster than the teamsters' wagons. Coaches averaged six to eight miles per hour on good roads, while the fastest passenger boats could only move five miles per hour on the Erie

Canal. However, most immigrants and western settlers, travelers with more time than money, turned gratefully to the canal for inexpensive transportation west.[5]

At first glance, the Erie Canal appears to have stimulated the growth of the population of Onondaga County. Between 1820 and 1830, the first decade of the canal's operation, the county's population increased 42 percent. This surpassed the rate of growth of the state of New York, which increased by 40 percent during the same decade, and of the nation, which grew by only 34 percent over the same ten years. Contemporary proponents of the canal pointed to the burgeoning population growth along the canal route as evidence that it brought prosperity and growth to the region, and early historians echoed this view. In 1900 Julius Winden articulated most fully the viewpoint that the canal laid the basis for population expansion and agricultural prosperity in western New York. His arguments were picked up a few years later by Noble E. Whitford, an engineer who was himself a strong advocate of canal transportation in general and the successor to the Erie Canal, the New York State Barge Canal, in particular. Whitford's two-volume *History of the Canal System of the State of New York*, using Winden's analysis to show the importance of the canal to population growth in western New York, remains the standard work on the canal.[6]

Unfortunately, neither study distinguished between rural and urban areas and neither was apparently cognizant of what was at first a relative and later an absolute decline in the rural population of these areas as the urban population climbed ever higher. More specifically, the 42 percent growth rate for Onondaga County disguises radically different rates of growth in various parts of the county. Canal-induced changes in traffic patterns simultaneously caused the rapid growth of settlements located along the canal and the concomitant economic and population decline of the previously healthy turnpike settlements. In effect, the center of population in Onondaga shifted northward during the 1820s from the tier of towns along the Seneca Turnpike (Manlius, Onondaga, and Marcellus) to the settlements along the canal (Manlius, Salina, Camillus, and Elbridge), with the greatest population growth occurring in the township of Salina at the center of the county and the southern end of Onondaga Lake. The township, which included the canal center of Syracuse as well as the three salt springs villages, increased its population by 282 percent during the 1820s, while the other townships in the county together grew by a mere 31 percent—or less than the national average.[7] (See Figure 5.)

The phenomenal population explosion of the township of Salina was caused by the combination of the new interregional transportation system with a staple export, salt, and thus was reflected in the three growing villages within its borders. After the construction of

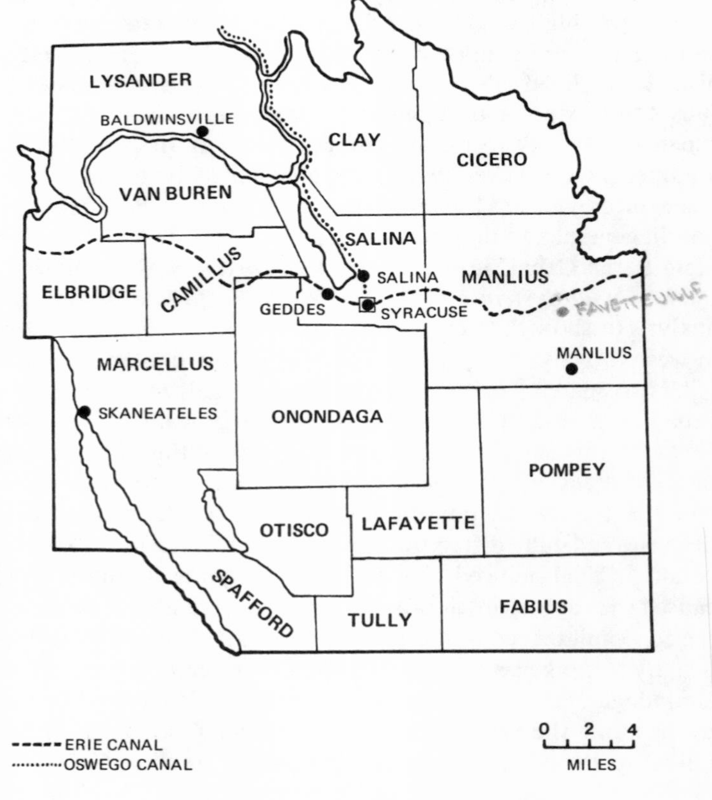

Figure 5. Onondaga County with the Erie Canal and the Oswego Canal, 1829

the canal, the economies of the three, Salina, Liverpool, and Geddes, continued to be based primarily on salt making. They changed, however, from little more than mining camps to villages with a more diversified economy. In the first four years after the opening of the middle section of the canal, Liverpool doubled in size, increasing from a settlement with twenty-five dwellings to one with fifty houses, twenty-five salt works, and a school. Geddes became almost as large by 1824, with forty-five houses, twelve to fourteen salt works, and a school. The schools themselves symbolized the changing composition of these communities, for prior to 1820 the population of the salt villages was largely composed of adult males. However the population too became more diversified following the construction of the Erie Canal, and women and soon children joined the salt boilers in these villages.[8]

Despite the growth of Geddes and Liverpool—and the somewhat slower growth of the larger village of Salina—the enormous 282 percent increase in the population of the township of Salina during the 1820s was primarily concentrated in the village of Syracuse. Located south of the town of Salina and east of Geddes at the junction of the Erie Canal, the North Branch of the Seneca or Genesee Turnpike, and the road north from Onondaga Hollow (see Figure 5), the site appeared unpromising in 1820. An unhealthy swamp caused by the overflow of Onondaga Lake lay between the few houses and cabins in the community and the lake. Residents succumbed to a "bilious fever" so severe that during the warmest months of the year many left the area to escape illness. Under the stimulus of a major landowner in the canal settlement, the swamp was drained in 1822 by enlarging the outlet to the lake and thus lowering the water level of Onondaga Lake. This cleared the way for the expansion of the village and facilitated road construction within the county to the new settlement. By 1824 Syracuse was already as large as Liverpool, and although it had no salt works as yet, several were planned for the following summer. More important, one of the five weighlocks on the Erie Canal was located at Syracuse. * Slowing and often stopping canal traffic in the settlement created an artificial break in transportation which, although not necessarily involving a transfer from one type of transportation to another, was a likely site for the location of urban economic activities.[9]

* The present CANAL MUSEUM.

Confirmation of the local importance of the growing canal village came in 1829 when the county buildings were moved from Onondaga West Hill, a turnpike village, to Syracuse. This transfer of the county seat brought a company of lawyers and county officials into the town previously settled by canal travelers, shippers, and salt boilers. By 1830, the population of Syracuse had risen to 2,565 people—an increase of 926 percent during the decade. Syracuse was now the largest settlement in the county.

In addition to Syracuse and the Salina salt settlements, other canal villages were also flourishing in the decade following the opening of the Erie Canal. Jordan, located on the canal in the township of Camillus, grew rapidly, drawing both population and customers from the village of Elbridge which was located on the turnpike, a few miles south of Jordan. Similarly, Canton drew business away from Ionia, an earlier settlement in the town of Camillus with a good turnpike location but not on the route of the canal, and the canal village of Fayetteville attracted a great deal of trade from Manlius Village. New villages also appeared at this time in the township of Manlius. For example, Kirkville, which began as a tavern on the canal, later attracted settlers because of its advantageous location; soon a store was added and, in 1824, a post office was established. The growth of canal villages like Kirkville in the early 1820s was partly a result of the influx of canal construction workers whose cash wages generated a local market for village services, agricultural products, and manufactured goods. These workers often remained in Onondaga County after they finished their work, usually settling in the canal towns.[10]

If the villages near the canal prospered in the 1820s, other Onondaga settlements fared less well. With the opening of the canal, settlements located on the turnpikes lost much of their business. Local businessmen deserted the turnpike villages for canal settlements—the most attractive of which was Syracuse. For example, even before the county courthouse and jail were moved to Syracuse in 1829, the settlement acquired two newspapers which were formerly published at Onondaga Hollow and Onondaga West Hill. Merchants, millers, and inn keepers, like the newspaper editors, saw a better future in Syracuse and left the turnpike villages for the rapidly growing canal village. Even Baldwinsville, a village in

Lysander located on the Seneca River, experienced an economic decline when traffic from the river was diverted to the canal. In short, the drying up of turnpike and river trade brought a temporary halt to village growth in areas off the Erie Canal, and most county villages, like the once-prosperous settlements of Jamesville and Pompey, were no larger in 1824 than they had been in 1813.[11]

Manlius Village, which became simply Manlius in the 1820s, provides a good illustration of the fate of the turnpike settlements after the construction of the canal. It was the most flourishing village in the county prior to 1820, and as late as 1822 an atlas of the state of New York named it as the most important settlement in Onondaga County in terms of wealth, population, buildings, and trade. When the future Whig and Republican politician Thurlow Weed moved to Onondaga County in 1820 to start a newspaper, he came to Manlius. Yet even as he made arrangements to take over the printing press of his predecessor, Weed was cautioned against expecting too much business in Manlius because it had been bypassed by the canal and was already losing its trade. Within a year, Weed had to admit that his advisers were correct; although the circulation of his paper was large, it received only limited advertising and Weed could not make enough to support his family. In 1822 he wisely left Manlius for Rochester. Those who stayed in Manlius only witnessed continued decline. As one resident noted in 1827, the village had "an old, dilapidated, forlorn look... The construction of the Erie Canal, although highly beneficial to the county in general, had a very injurious effect upon the business of this village. It opened new avenues for commerce, and invited enterprise and activity to other geographical points." Azariah Smith, a leading merchant, made the same observation in writing to his father in 1830. "We have found," he wrote, "uniformly since the canal opened, a falling off in our business." At that time the population of the village was only 989, compared with an estimated population of 1,500 eight years earlier.[12]

Attempts to fight the economically debilitating competition of the canal villages centered upon construction of auxiliary canals. In 1825, residents of Manlius proposed that a feeder canal be built from the village to the Erie Canal, a distance of four miles. They felt that farmers to the south would be interested in an auxiliary waterway that would save four miles of travel to the Erie Canal and give the farmers a market in Manlius. "If we succeed in getting our side cut," a village businessman wrote, "we think that we shall still be able to cope with our neighboring village on the canal." Manlius was not alone in seeking to build feeder canals, for additional waterways were proposed to and from the canal by nearly all major villages in Onondaga County and neighboring non-canal counties. The only additional canal to be built in the county, however, was the Oswego Canal, which served interregional rather than local purposes.[13]

The failure of what were now backcountry villages to stem the exodus of businesses to the canal route settlements resulted in a gradual deterioration of other, non-canal transportation facilities throughout the county. In addition to the loss of traffic on the county turnpikes, small local roads were also used less frequently because they had been built for a traffic pattern oriented toward turnpike villages rather than canal settlements. As a result, hamlets that had grown up along these local roads settled into the same stupor which affected the larger villages along the turnpikes. Snow Bridge, a toll bridge built in 1811 over the Seneca River in the northwestern part of the county, was abandoned in 1830 because competition from the Erie Canal had caused its traffic to diminish. Moreover, the major water route to the east prior to 1820—along the Seneca River and Oneida Lake—was rarely if ever used after the canal was built. Boats laden with goods for the West and for Canada had passed there frequently before 1820, but with few cargo shipments across the lake after the canals were opened, boat landings on Oneida Lake were left commercially useless.[14]

The economic decline in the villages located away from the Erie Canal in the early 1820s was paralleled by a decline in the population growth of the non-canal townships, a decline which appeared particularly stark next to the burgeoning growth of the new canal settlement of Syracuse. Differences in population growth between Syracuse and the rest of the county suggest that the growth of the city and its hinterland be examined separately, for despite differences among Onondaga townships by 1825, they—and the villages within them—were more like each other than like Syracuse. Even the canal villages outside Syracuse experienced a decline in the rate of population growth by the late 1820s. For example, within the township of Salina itself, the rate of growth of Liverpool and Geddes declined from an increase of approximately 150 percent in both villages between 1813 and 1824 to 20 percent and 11 percent, respectively, between 1824 and 1836.

The population trends of the 1820s continued into the following decade. Between 1830 and 1840, the population of the entire county grew by only 15 percent, comparing unfavorably with the 27 percent increase experienced by the state of New York and 33 percent increase of the entire United States. Most of Onondaga County's increase was still concentrated in Syracuse, which grew by 144 percent. The county hinterland of the canal city grew only 9 percent—far below the national average rural population increase of 30 percent—and a number of Onondaga townships actually declined in population during this decade. These included both Spafford and Fabius, which had 29 percent and 17 percent fewer people in 1840 than in 1830; Pompey and Otisco, which declined by 9 percent and 2 percent; and Salina (excluding Syracuse) whose population was 9 percent smaller in 1840 than it had been in 1830. While the large population loss in Spafford was undoubtedly due to a contraction in the township's borders, the other townships remained the same size during the decade. The slowing growth—and occasional decline—of the population of most of the county outside Syracuse is indicative of the growing divergence between Syracuse and its hinterland. (See Figure 6.)

Measurement of net population change, however, does not indicate the extent of in-migration, out-migration, or natural increase—any combination of which could be responsible for population changes. To do this, it is possible to estimate the crude rate of natural increase, compare this to actual population change, and calculate an estimated net migration rate as a residual. This calculation can be made for the mid-decade years when the state census was taken, for births and deaths in each township were fortunately recorded by the state census takers along with total population figures.

Using these estimates of natural increase and net migration, we can examine population change in the township of Salina separately from that of the rest of the county. Ideally Syracuse should

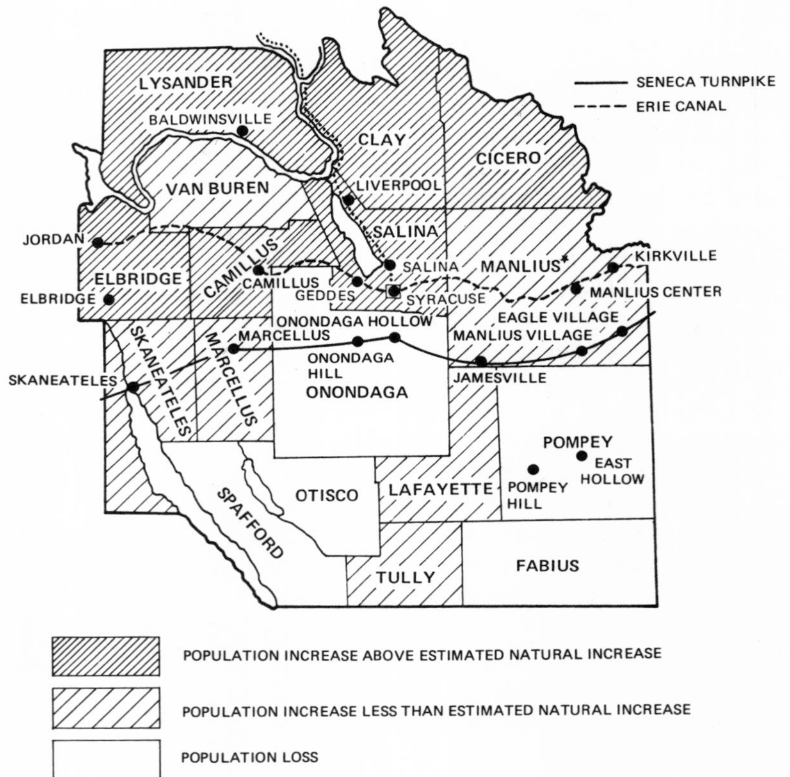

SOURCE: United States Census, 1830 and 1840

Figure 6. Population Change in Onondaga County, 1830-1840

be separated from the other parts of the township of Salina, but since the crude rate of natural increase can only be calculated on the basis of births and deaths recorded by township, it is not possible to calculate this rate for smaller units within townships.

While the estimated crude rate of natural increase for the township of Salina did not correspond exactly to that of Syracuse, the figure was strongly influenced by the growing city, for the population of Syracuse was more than one-third of the township's population in 1830 and over one-half its population by 1840. The bias introduced by the inclusion of the entire township in a single estimated rate of natural increase would tend to minimize rather than exaggerate the differences between Syracuse and the hinterland because the slower growth of the township outside the city was closer to the hinterland growth pattern than it was to that of Syracuse.[15]

As the proportional rate of increase indicates, Salina and its principal settlement Syracuse received more migrants than did the hinterland during the two decades following the construction of the Erie Canal. The expected crude rate of natural increase in Salina was 25.8 percent for the 1820s. (See Table 3.1.) Given the overall population growth of 282 percent, we can estimate that in-migration exceeded out-migration by 256 percent. Most of the in-migration to Salina went to Syracuse, for if we apply the expected crude rate of natural increase for the decade of the 1820s separately to Syracuse and to the remainder of Salina, we find that Salina with an overall growth of 179 percent must have had a net in-migration

Table 3.1. **Crude Rate of Natural Increase (in percent)**

	1825	1835
Annual Crude Rate of Natural Increase		
Onondaga County	2.8	2.3
Salina	2.3	2.7
County hinterland	2.8	2.2
Estimated Crude Rate of Natural Increase by Decade		
	1820-1830	1830-1840
Onondaga County	31.6	25.4
Salina	25.8	30.9
County hinterland	32.1	24.6

SOURCE: New York State Census, 1825 and 1835.

for the decade of 153 percent while Syracuse, with a much higher population increase of 926, had a surplus of in-migrants totaling at least 900 percent.

In the hinterland townships, out-migration was slightly higher than in-migration. With an expected crude rate of natural increase of 32.1 percent, the hinterland was far more fertile than the more urban township of Salina during the 1820s. Moreover, this expected natural increase in the hinterland was slightly higher than the actual population increase, indicating that out-migration from the townships of the county hinterland in the 1820s exceeded in-migration. There were some variations in hinterland migration patterns. As might be expected, out-migration was greatest in the parts of the county that had been settled earliest. In Spafford and Lysander, two townships which were considerably less densely settled than the rest of the county, in-migration exceeded out-migration by 73 percent and 53 percent, although even here in-migration did not approach the scale of in-migration to Salina.

In the following decade, in-migration to Salina, principally to Syracuse, continued to exceed in-migration to the rest of the county. By the end of the 1830s, the township of Salina had 133 men for each 100 women in the 20-to-40 age group. The heavy preponderance of men is typical of an area of in-migration, for males, particularly young adult males, are more likely to migrate than are women of the same age. Yet Syracuse was not merely a magnet for young men; it was increasingly becoming an area of family settlement. This is indicated by Salina's changing crude rate of natural increase which rose from 25.8 percent in the 1820s to 30.9 percent in the 1830s. Moreover, in-migration to Syracuse continued to exceed the natural increase of 113 percent in the population of the city in the 1830s. Out-migration exceeded in-migration in the rest of the township of Salina, which experienced an absolute population loss of 9 percent and a probable net out-migration of 40 percent of the 1830 population by 1840. By the 1830s, migration patterns in rural and village Salina were more similar to those of the county hinterland than to those of Syracuse. With an estimated crude rate of natural increase of 24.6 for the decade, the county hinterland experienced an estimated net out-migration of 15 percent of its 1830 population by 1840.[16]

The rise in out-migration from Onondaga County in the 1830s was undoubtedly related to the nationwide movement to western lands which peaked in 1830. The corresponding drop in the growth rates of city and hinterland in the decade shows that both areas were affected by the western competition. However the urban area continued to grow despite its diminished growth rate while the county hinterland began to lose population.

The decline in rural populations has been noted elsewhere. Whitney R. Cross ascribed the out-migration of rural populations in western New York to the area's having reached a "rural saturation point," which he estimated at about sixty people per square mile. More recently, Richard A. Easterlin has suggested that after the period of initial settlement, fertility began to decline throughout all northern agricultural areas in the nineteenth century. This decline in fertility was followed, somewhat later, by out-migration. Both phenomena, according to Easterlin, are due to the desire of farmers to provide financially for each of their children. In the face of rising land prices, farm families had fewer children in settled areas than they had in frontier areas where land was cheaper and more readily available.[17]

However, the population was not declining in all parts of the county hinterland, for in the 1830s there was an important increase in the proportion of the population living in villages, including the non-canal villages which were finally beginning to recover from the malaise that had enveloped them after the Erie Canal was opened to traffic in 1820. Although these villages lost population as well as businesses in the 1820s, they were experiencing new growth by the 1830s. In 1824, only 7 percent of the county's population outside of the township of Salina lived in villages. By 1836 this figure had risen to 16 percent, and in five townships more than 20 percent of the population resided in villages. The growth in the village component of township populations in the 1830s was due to a combination of rural out-migration and village in-migration. Hinterland residents became less isolated as more people chose to live in concentrated residential settlements than had been the case even ten years earlier.[18] (See Table 3.2.)

The nature of the population expansion in hinterland villages suggests that their new population growth in the 1830s was related

Table 3.2. **Percentage of Township Population in Villages**

	1824	1836
Camillus	—	14
Cicero	—	4
Clay	*	—
DeWitt	*	14
Elbridge	*	32
Fabius	—	7
LaFayette	*	5
Lysander	5	27
Manlius	16	22
Marcellus	11	21
Onondaga	14	14
Otisco	—	7
Pompey	10	11
Salina	35	56
Skaneateles	*	42
Spafford	—	9
Tully	—	8
VanBuren	*	8

SOURCE: New York State Census, 1825 and 1835; Spafford, *Gazetteer* (1824); Gordon, *Gazetteer* (1836).

*In 1824, these townships were part of another township.

to general economic changes in the hinterland. Village population growth was largely due to the in-migration of middle-aged and elderly people rather than to an increase in the number of children or young people. The village of Manlius, located south of the Erie Canal in Manlius township, illustrates this process. Between 1830 and 1840, the number of people over the age of 40 increased both absolutely and in comparison with the rest of the population. The absolute growth of this age group was in large part the result of the aging of the village population. The corresponding rise in the proportion of the population over 40 also indicates that the size of the younger age groups was not growing as quickly as that of their elders. There were proportionately fewer young adults between the ages of 20 and 30 and fewer children under the age of 10 in 1840 than there had been in 1830. In fact, the cohort between the ages of

20 and 30 in 1830 was only 56 percent as large in 1840 as it had been ten years earlier. This rapid change suggests that young adults in Manlius, as in other parts of the hinterland, were moving out of the village in greater numbers than were other age groups and also that fewer people of this age were migrating into the village to replace those who emigrated. By the last half of the 1830s, the population decline among adults of childbearing age had affected the total number of births, and by 1840 there was a drop in the number of children under the age of 5.[19] (See Table 3.3.)

Table 3.3. **Manlius Village Population by Age, 1830 and 1840 (in percent)**

	1830		1840	
	Male	*Female*	*Male*	*Female*
Under 10	27	27	29	20
10 to 20	25	31	25	35
20 to 30	22	19	17	17
30 to 40	13	11	10	11
40 to 50	9	8	10	9
50 to 60	4	3	6	4
60 and over	1	2	4	4
Total	101*	101*	101*	100
N	471	517	449	600

SOURCE: "Town of Manlius and Vicinity."

*Figures here and in the following tables may not total 100 percent because of rounding.

The shift from rural to village residences, affecting where people lived and where they worked, is evidence of structural changes taking place in the hinterland economy. Uncovering the pattern of these changes, however, is complicated by the inadequacies of available data, particularly agricultural data in the years from 1820 to 1840. There are no figures on agricultural production in the county or even estimates of acreage devoted to specific crops before 1845, and the only time series available gives the numbers of various kinds of livestock and the total number of improved acres per township. With industrial changes during this period, we are on somewhat firmer ground, if only because the New York State census recorded the kinds of industry, and often the profits, in each township in the county.

Despite the paucity of agricultural data, several observations are possible. The Erie Canal gave an initial impetus to agriculture in the county by making the national markets more accessible to Onondaga farmers. Although by 1820 farmers were already dependent upon the national market in wheat, cured meat, and whiskey, markets were scattered and transportation by sleigh or turnpike was expensive. In addition, farmers and the general merchants from small county villages who frequently marketed their customers' produce did not have the regular, sustained contact with urban wholesalers necessary to demand the most favorable prices or fair treatment. The opening of the canal enabled farmers to raise their profits by cutting transportation costs. Equally important, marketing patterns gradually changed after the Erie Canal was opened. The canal established a single route for interregional marketing of agricultural produce and solidified the market dominance of New York City over the smaller urban markets in central New York state where Onondaga farmers had frequently traded earlier.

Syracuse, which had assumed salt marketing leadership from Salina because of its superior canal location, then became a commercial center for agriculture as well. The growing city boasted both physical and informational access to the New York market by virtue of its transportation functions. The Syracuse papers carried advertisements calling for agricultural products throughout the county. In time, commission agents and forwarders based in Syracuse replaced hinterland merchants and farmers in marketing the products of Onondaga agriculture. Buyers and agents included local urban dry goods and grocery merchants with storage facilities who offered farmers either cash or goods for produce, and forwarding and commission agents who were eager to market county grain. Not only were Syracuse forwarders able to ensure regular shipments and favorable prices, but the volume of business they attracted from Onondaga and the surrounding counties resulted in the construction of additional warehouses and storage facilities in Syracuse. This had a multiplier effect on the city's economy, expanding employment in a number of areas outside the simple management and promotion of interregional trade.[20]

Farmers responded to these changes in marketing patterns and transportation costs by expanding their holdings, thus increasing production. As a result, the number of acres of improved farm land in the county almost doubled between 1820 and 1835. Livestock holdings also increased, with 38 percent more sheep and 35 percent more cattle raised in the county in the first five years of the canal's operation than had been raised in 1820. Sheep grazing was increasing thoughout the North at this time and the jump in the number of sheep in Onondaga County indicates that Onondagans were responsive to national agricultural trends.[21]

Ironically, the market advantages of the Erie Canal which induced Onondaga farmers to increase production also led to an unexpected crisis in Onondaga agriculture by the late 1830s. First, the decline in the condition of local roads which followed the rush of interregional transportation to the canal made local transportation more inefficient than it had been. Trips from the farm to the canal were now often the most difficult part of getting crops to market. As a result, farmers and merchants still had to wait until the snow fell to transport their produce to the canal by sleigh.

Far more important than the weather, however, were the shipments of agricultural products which were beginning to come across the canal from the newly settled states around the Great Lakes. These products, particularly wheat and wool, directly and successfully competed with the products of the farms of central New York State. Some critics even claimed in 1840 that farmers a few miles from the canal had to pay more for transportation than did farmers in Ohio and Michigan who could ship their wheat entirely by water. Moreover, western wheat could be grown much more cheaply than New York wheat because the land itself was cheaper and the soil better, yielding more bushels of wheat per acre than the now tired lands of New York. The first shipments of wheat from Ohio arrived in the early 1830s, and by 1847 more than half the agricultural produce shipped on the Erie Canal came from the western states.[22]

In addition to competing with western farmers, Onondaga farmers were, by the late 1830s, also forced to contend with declining wheat yields and, as a result, declining agricultural profits. In Onondaga County, as in many American frontier areas, the land was first planted with wheat as a commercial crop regardless of whether the soil could better support other crops or even grazing. A visitor to the southern part of the county in 1824, noting the area's concentration on grains, remarked: "There is grain, and grass land, but as the general character [of the land] indicates dairy and stock farming, I would repeat. . . that the people of this State have a strange and blind attachment to grain farming, and to such an extent, that it operates very much to the detriment of the general interests of the community." Once the wheat was planted, moreover, farmers did little to improve the soil other than planting clover and occasionally applying gypsum. Their methods of cultivation, called "skimming" by a local agricultural expert, exhausted the soil. George Geddes, a resident who was more interested in scientific farming than were most Onondagans, noted in 1843 that even his land had been farmed "more with a view to see when the soil would be exhausted, than how fine crops could be obtained, or how the most money could be realized."[23]

The farmers' difficulties were further complicated by the increase in the number of farmers in the county between 1820 and 1840. Although land newly open to cultivation was partly absorbed by local farmers, it also attracted additional farmers to the county. Moreover, while the number of acres of improved land nearly doubled by 1835, as we have seen, there were also 69 percent more farmers in the county in 1840 than there had been when the canal was opened in 1820. As a result, the number of acres of improved land per farmer rose only slightly, from 20.9 to 24.8 acres, and much of the gain was in marginal lands. Individual farms were larger than this, however, because many farmers did not own land but instead worked for other farmers. The crowded and discouraging agricultural prospects of the county together with the inflation in the cost of farmland in canal counties probably contributed as much to the large rural out-migration of the 1830s as did the positive attractions of western land.

Despite the increase in the total number of farmers in Onondaga County, the proportion of the county's employed work force engaged in agriculture declined between 1820 and 1840 because of the rapid growth of the urban work force in Syracuse and the larger villages. In 1820, 80 percent of the county's employed work force were farmers, but by 1840 the proportion had shrunk to 64 percent or less than two-thirds of the work force. Predictably, the urban township of Salina had the lowest proportion of farmers with only 23 percent of its work force employed in agriculture in 1840. Outside of Salina, the work force in hinterland townships ranged from 79 percent to 95 percent farmers in 1820, when their economies were almost totally dominated by agriculture, and from 51 percent to 85 percent in 1840.

Although the proportion of farmers declined in all hinterland townships over the twenty-year period, townships without large villages generally had as large a proportion of the work force engaged in agriculture in 1840 as the mean of all townships in 1820. However by 1840, they had a somewhat smaller proportion engaged in manufacturing than was common in 1820 and a slightly larger proportion engaged in commerce than they had twenty years earlier. These agricultural townships without large villages had no direct access to the Erie Canal and were losing population. Their economies were increasingly characterized by the absence of local industry and the dominance of agriculture.

The impact of the construction of the Erie Canal and the consequent growth of the city of Syracuse not only had a deleterious effect upon the agricultural economy of Onondaga County, but it also had a disruptive effect upon the county's industries. By 1820 Onondaga had a fairly diversified industrial base with both extractive export industries and rural processing and manufacturing industries. The opening of the canal promised to expand the market for the county's mineral resources, salt, and gypsum. In fact, not only did the canal enhance the possibilities for the sale of salt and gypsum, but canal construction itself also provided a market for Onondaga water lime (limestone) and granite. At the same time, however, the opening of a low-cost interregional transportation system and the shipment of large quantities of agricultural goods along a single route led to the construction along the canal of larger processing facilities than were feasible earlier. The resulting decline of the small rural processing industries, particularly in canal-crossed townships, was accompanied by the usurpation of manufacturing by urban and village interests.

More positively, the most immediate effect of the opening of the Erie Canal was the expansion of the market for Onondaga salt. In the first five years of the canal's operation, before the entire canal was completed, salt production increased by an average of 70,492 bushels each year as compared to an average annual increase of only 30,004 bushels from 1810 to 1820. Between 1826 and 1830, with the added transportation advantages of the fully completed Erie Canal and the Oswego Canal, salt production increased by an average of 105,060 bushels annually. Shipment by canal facilitated the growth of salt markets as far away as Chicago and Cincinnati and gave Onondaga salt a competitive advantage in eastern urban markets over imported salt, which had previously dominated the coastal markets. Nor did Onondaga salt makers lose or ignore their markets located off the Erie Canal, for salt continued to be shipped north by the Oswego Canal after 1828, and south through the Susquehanna River system to markets which were far from any canal. The result was a continued expansion of salt production in the canal period. Both the settlements around the salt springs and the county hinterland benefited from the growth of the salt market. As the county's major export industry, the salt works were able to provide relatively steady, if seasonal, employment for residents of the salt springs villages. An industrial spin-off of the expanding salt industry in Syracuse, salt grinding, appeared in the city sometime after 1830.[24]

Shipping salt via the canal indirectly provided the county with investment capital. The revenues of the state's Canal Fund, a large proportion of which was made up of salt duties, were deposited in banks along the canal. This involved a sizable amount of capital: between 1817 and 1836, salt duties alone totaled over two million dollars. A large proportion of this money went to Syracuse banks where it was used for loans to city and hinterland residents until it was needed for canal-related expenses. The additional investment capital provided by salt duties was particularly important in a county such as Onondaga where there was a shortage of capital.[25]

The county hinterland benefited in still another way from the expansion of the salt industry made possible by the canal. While Salina itself first provided the necessary wood for boiling the salt water to obtain salt and the barrels for shipping the salt, its land was in time denuded and salt manufacturers had to turn to other parts of the county for wood. By the 1830s, they were dependent upon Lysander in the northwestern corner of the county for fuel for boiling the salt water; the timber was floated down the Oswego Canal to Salina. Similarly, Camillus, and later Clay and Cicero, replaced Salina in providing the barrels for the salt industry. The more specialized production of small wooden boxes for packing fine salt developed in the village of Geddes. Unfortunately, supplying the salt industry with barrels for shipment and wood for its fires were activities that depended upon an exhaustible resource and thus proved only a temporary and limited economic stimulus to the county hinterland. Profits, moreover, were low despite the assistance of the state of New York, which removed all canal tolls from lumber being shipped down the Oswego Canal to the salt springs.[26]

In addition to the market impact of the Erie Canal upon the salt industry, other extractive industries in Onondaga County were also directly dependent upon the canal. Onondaga limestone was first burned and then pulverized to make "American hydraulic cement." The process was discovered while the canal was being built and was subsequently used in its construction. Limestone for the cement was quarried and prepared for market in the towns of Manlius and DeWitt. Granite, used extensively in the construction of the Oswego Canal and the enlargement of the Erie Canal after 1835, was quarried in the nearby township of Onondaga about three- to four-and-a-half miles from the canal. Transporting granite the short distance from the quarries to the canal proved to be the major difficulty in using Onondaga granite for canal construction. When Onondaga granite was specified for use in building an aqueduct near Rochester, the engineers reported that even when the roads were in good condition, transportation costs from the quarries to the canal were at least half of the total cost of transportation from that point on the canal to the city of Rochester—a distance of ninety-eight miles. In 1836, a short-distance railroad was built to provide faster, more convenient transportation from the quarries to the canal. No auxiliary industries grew up around these extractive industries such as those which developed to service the salt industry. Consequently the multiplier effect on the local economy of quarrying granite and limestone was considerably less than that of the salt industry.[27]

Rural processing industries in Onondaga County were affected differently by the opening of the Erie Canal and the subsequent growth of Syracuse than were the extractive industries. The availability of low-cost canal transportation only contributed to the growth of residentiary processing industries when economies of scale, provided by broadening the effective hinterland of a particular industry, enabled an industry to expand its operations appreciably. More often, interregional transportation efficiencies either eliminated the need for certain local processing industries or introduced successful competition from outside the region. The distilling industry, for example, was largely destroyed by the canal. To save transportation costs prior to 1820, farmers frequently converted their heavy grain into more easily transported whiskey before shipping it to eastern markets. With the canal, transportation costs for grain were so low that distillation became unnecessary, and the fifty distilleries in Onondaga County in 1825 shrank in number to eleven in 1835 and to six in 1845.

Similarly, gristmills were no longer as important in preparing grain for shipment as they had been earlier, for the change from turnpikes or sleighs to canal boats for interregional marketing encouraged the shipment of the heavier whole grain rather than the lighter flour. Moreover, the expansion of wheat-growing land in western New York and the western states led to the development of large milling centers in western or canal port cities such as Rochester, Buffalo, and Oswego, usually at points of transfer from one type of interregional transportation to another. These factors, along with the local decline in wheat production, interrupted the expansion of the local custom mills in Onondaga County. In 1825, there were fifty-six grist mills in the county, almost half of which were located in the townships of Manlius and Marcellus. After this, however, there were fewer grist mills reported in operation at every census.[28]

Outside competition hurt the saw mills in Onondaga County much less than it hurt the grist mills. For at least a decade and a half after the Erie Canal was opened, the growing city of Syracuse devoured lumber for its new houses and stores while its salt works, as we have seen, were also increasingly dependent upon county forest products for both making and marketing salt. Lumber, barrels, and firewood could be acquired more cheaply in the county than imported from outside it, and the lumber industry in Onondaga County expanded as Syracuse and the salt market expanded. At the time the canal was first opened in 1820, there were ninety-nine saw mills; fifteen years later their number had reached 162. Milling was extremely profitable at this time. The abundance of wood in the county made it possible to locate saw mills near the heaviest concentrations of population, and in 1820, the correlation between the number of saw mills in a township and the township's population was +.938. As the demand for lumber increased, new mills were constructed in the less heavily populated townships where good supplies of timber were still available, and by 1830, the correlation between population and saw mills had disappeared (+.044). Profits, or the value added to lumber by processing, began to decline in Onondaga mills after 1835 and the total number of saw mills in the county declined as well. By 1855, there were only eighty-one mills left, the smallest number since the advent of the canal. However, the sharp drop in the number of saw mills was due as much to the disappearance of large stands of good wood in the county as to the fall in profits, for other processing industries dependent upon wood, such as the tanneries and asheries, also began to disappear around the same time.[29]

Another local industry which declined during the first twenty years of the canal's operation was the home manufacture of textiles and the carding and fulling mills which finished home-produced cloth. While the Seneca Turnpike and later the growth of Syracuse itself appear to have exerted some influence upon the demise of the home manufacture of cloth, the Erie Canal and the Erie and Oswego canal system after 1828 were a more potent force. The crucial factor in this decline was distance from the canals. The same pattern that Rolla Tryon found among all counties in New York State can be found among townships within a county; townships or counties at some distance from the Erie Canal continued to produce home-manufactured textiles longer than townships or counties close to the canal. In 1825, the correlation between distance from the turnpike and the number of yards of home-manufactured cloth per person by township was +.463, while the association between per capita cloth production and distance from the Erie

Canal was +.851. Similarly in 1835, the correlation between per capita cloth production and distance from the Erie Canal was +.820 and from the Erie and Oswego Canals, +.713; the correlation between distance from the growing commercial center of Syracuse and cloth production in households in 1835 was only +.417. In short, home manufacture of textiles was more strongly associated with distance from the canals, which was related to total population, than with distance from Syracuse. Individuals living in the more populous townships located on or near the canals were less dependent upon home manufactured cloth than were those who lived farther away from the canals. The carding machines and fulling mills did custom work for farm families that produced cloth, and as the demand for their services slackened, they gradually disappeared from the county.[30]

As agricultural processing industries became less important a part of the county's economy, the locational pattern of county industry also changed. Industry was scattered throughout Onondaga County in 1820, frequently in rural locations and always near good sources of water power. By the late 1820s and early 1830s, however, industry became increasingly concentrated in Syracuse and the major county villages. The concentration of industrial activity in population centers was analogous to the process of population coalescence which was taking place at the same time. The dispersed rural settlement pattern of the pre-canal period gave way to the now familiar agricultural settlement pattern characterized by large multi-purpose villages surrounded by farm lands inhabited only by the farmers themselves. Residentiary rural industry and isolated crossroads stores became less important as the growing villages took over their commercial and processing functions and as interregional marketing changes made other functions obsolete or no longer necessary. Townships without sizable villages became more completely dominated by agriculture and between 1820 and 1840 experienced a decline in the proportion of the work force engaged in manufacturing.[31]

By 1840, many of the county's industries were located in Syracuse, which enjoyed the advantages of an interregional transportation and supply system, a sizable population for employment, access to a growing regional market, and capital for investment. As early as 1835, the city functioned as an industrial as well as a transportation and marketing center for the county. Although the population of Syracuse was then only 4,103, there were sixteen factories and three machine shops, exclusive of extractive and processing industries. The small size of these industries and the diversity of their products, however, suggests that they developed in response to a variety of local or regional needs rather than as a means to exploit a particular export product for the interregional market. Other manufacturing centers in the county at this time were the villages of Jordan, Baldwinsville, and Skaneateles, and, to a lesser extent, Manlius and Marcellus. None of these settlements, however, had as much as one-third the manufacturing capacity of Syracuse.[32]

Eric E. Lampard has suggested that the specialization of economic functions which accompanies industrialization causes territorial divisions in economic activity between town and country. However the areal specialization in industrial activity taking place in Onondaga County between 1820 and 1840 did not involve significant changes in industrial processes or scale. Urban and village industry in the county differed little from rural industry in terms of its technology or the organization of production. Instead, the changing locus of industrial activity at this time was the result of alterations in interregional marketing patterns. Commercial, rather than industrial or technological, changes were responsible for the growing tendency for county industry to be located in the city and the villages rather than in the rural areas in which it was so often found before the canal was built.[33]

The role of the canal in the growth of manufacturing in the West in the period 1820 to 1840 has been the subject of a debate between Albert W. Niemi, Jr., and Roger L. Ransom. Throughout their exchange, however, they discuss manufacturing in the entire western section of the northern United States without accounting for urban and rural differences within this large region or within smaller subareas such as counties. Urban and rural differences are essential to a study of industry during this period, for it was at this time that the location of industrial activity began to shift perceptibly from rural to village and urban locations. In time, residentiary processing industries declined and, as we shall see in the next chapter, were gradually replaced in hinterland villages by industries that manufactured items needed by local agriculture. The market for these growing urban manufacturers, however, generally remained local, not national.[34]

Urban and rural differences in terms of the location of industrial activity was just one of the changes which occurred in Onondaga County after the opening of the Erie Canal. The population of the county had risen from roughly 41,000 to almost 68,000, and the distribution of the population within the county had altered markedly. Pre-canal villages that had grown up along the turnpike went through a period of economic decline when interregional traffic shifted northward from turnpike to canal. The growth of these villages stopped abruptly and many village businesses floundered, while at the same time Syracuse, the infant settlement at the weighlock of the canal and later the junction of the Erie and Oswego Canals, experienced rapid growth. Though legally still a village, Syracuse, with over 6,000 people, was a city in all other ways by 1840. Outside Syracuse, however, the growth rate of the county hinterland declined and some townships experienced an absolute population decline.

Syracuse and Salina were followed in size and importance in 1840 by Skaneateles, Jordan, Manlius, and Baldwinsville—second-level villages which were scattered throughout the county. With populations well over 1,000 each, these settlements were all much larger than the major county villages of 1813 and 1824. Despite the declining growth rate of the hinterland population in the 1830s, these settlements had recovered from the earlier competition of the canal villages and were thriving by the end of the decade. Their growth was evidence of the change in rural settlement patterns from the pre-canal dispersal of both agricultural and industrial populations to a pattern of agricultural settlement in the hinterland punctuated by large villages which combined commercial and industrial activities. In part, these second-level villages in 1840 owed their recent growth to locational advantages in the growing regional transportation network, which was made up of the Erie and Oswego Canals, local and regional turnpikes, and access roads to the canals. A further advantage possessed by these settlements was good water power sites. For example, Jordan enjoyed a favorable location on the Erie Canal which provided both transportation and water power from the overflow of the canal. Baldwinsville, which suffered in the years immediately following the opening of the Erie Canal, began to grow again with the construction of the Oswego Canal, which gave it direct access to the Seneca River. Baldwinsville also took advantage of its excellent water power facilities to such an extent that contemporaries called it an industrial village. Skaneateles, although bypassed by the Erie Canal, was located on several important turnpikes along which most of the agricultural products from counties south of Onondaga were shipped to the canal. A local milling center, it produced nearly 40,000 barrels of flour in 1830. Manlius was located upon other, though less important, regional turnpikes leading to the Erie waterway. Both Skaneateles and Manlius also boasted good water power sites.[35]

In addition to changes in settlement patterns and in the location of industrial activity, the canal also contributed to the increasingly unstable condition of agriculture in the county in the 1830s. Originally having prospered because the canal provided low-cost transportation to eastern markets, Onondaga farmers faced growing western competition by 1840, also resulting from the canal. Their problems were compounded by declining wheat yields.

While the advent of the canal marked the beginning of many of these changes, it was not the canal that directly caused them. Certain of the changes that took place in this period had actually begun before the construction of the canal. There was, for example, an incipient multi-county regional trading system centering around the salt springs prior to 1820. The agricultural practices that led to the declining fertility of county wheat lands in the 1830s had already become part of the accepted way of cultivating wheat before the canal was built. However after 1820 the canal introduced a new element into the existing social and economic organization of the county that both delayed the development of intraregional trading systems in favor of interregional marketing and exacerbated the difficulties experienced by wheat farmers. The canal was, to be sure, a major stimulus to the county's development, but it was one which operated indirectly, setting in motion a series of interacting processes which actually effected the socioeconomic changes that occurred. The growth of Syracuse and the transformation of marketing patterns, permitted and encouraged by the availability of regular, low-cost interregional transportation, led to alterations in agricultural and industrial practices in Onondaga County. These, in turn, had important social ramifications, shaping both migration and settlement patterns. In the subsequent two decades, further transportation innovations and urban expansion were to intensify the tendencies that appeared in the 1830s and transform the county even more.

Notes

1. *Memorial of the Commissioners of the State of New York, in Behalf of said State; praying the Aid of the General Government of opening a Communication between Navigable Waters of Hudson River and the Lakes* (Washington: William A. Davis, 1816); Caroline E. MacGill, et al., *History of Transportation in the United States before 1860* (Washington: Carnegie Institute of Washington, 1917), p. 167; Nathan Miller, *The Enterprise of a Free People: Aspects of Economic Development during the Canal Period, 1792-1838* (Ithaca: Cornell University Press, 1962), pp. 34-40, 61; and Report of the Canal Commissioners, March 7, 1820, in *Laws of the State of New York, in relation to the Erie and Champlain Canals, together with the annual reports of the canal commissioners and other documents*, 2 vols. (Albany: E. E. Hosfor, 1825). For a general history of public works, see American Public Works Association, *History of Public Works in the United States, 1776-1976*, Ellis L. Armstrong, Michael C. Robinson, and Suellen Hoy, eds. (Chicago: American Public Works Association, 1976). Government support for public works is discussed in Robert A. Lively, "The American System: A Review Article," *Business History Review*, 29 (1955), 81-96.

2. MacGill, *History of Transportation*, pp. 189-190; *New York State Assembly Journal* (1820), p. 666; Miller, *Enterprise of a Free People*, p. 72; Joshua V. H. Clark, *Onondaga; or Reminiscences of Earlier and Later Times*, II (Syracuse: Stoddard and Babcock, 1849), pp. 88-90.

3. J. H. French, *Gazetteer of the State of New York*. . . (Syracuse: R. P. Smith, 1860), pp. 58-63.

4. *The Merchants' Magazine and Commercial Review*, V (September 1841), 284; Dwight H. Bruce, *Onondaga's Centennial: Gleanings of a Century*, I ([Boston]: Boston History Company, 1896), p. 222; Whitney R. Cross, "Creating a City: Rochester, 1824-1834" (M.A. thesis, University of Rochester, 1936), pp. 65-66; and George Rogers Taylor, *The Transportation Revolution, 1815-1860* (New York: Holt, Rinehart and Winston, 1951), pp. 138, 142.

5. Bruce, *Onondaga's Centennial*, I, p. 222; and Taylor, *The Transportation Revolution*, p. 142.

6. Winden's work, through Whitford's adaptation, has remained the standard interpretation of the role of the Erie Canal in New York since 1906. Most recently the same arguments have been reiterated by Ronald E. Shaw in *Erie Water West: A History of the Erie Canal, 1792-1854* (Lexington: University of Kentucky Press, 1966). See also Julius Winden, "The Influence of the Erie Canal upon the Population along its Course" (B.Ph. thesis, University of Wisconsin, 1900), and Noble E. Whitford, *History of the Canal System of the State of New York*, 2 vols., Supplement to the Annual Report of the State Engineer and Surveyor of the State of New York, 1905 (Albany: Brandow Printing Co., 1906).

7. Population data are taken from the United States Census, 1820, 1830, and 1840. Population growth was reflected in political boundary changes between 1825 and 1835 which subdivided the larger townships in Onondaga County. Camillus was divided into three parts in 1829, Van Buren in the north, Elbridge in the southwest, and Camillus in the southeast. Pompey lost its western half in 1825 when LaFayette was established, and Marcellus was similarly divided in 1830 when Skaneateles was formed. The last boundary change in the first two decades of the canal's operation was in the township of Manlius, split vertically into Manlius and DeWitt in 1835. The effect of these changes was to make the townships, with the exception of Salina, more nearly equal in terms of area and population.

8. Horatio Gates Spafford, *A Gazetteer of the State of New York* (Albany: H. C. Southwick, 1813); and Horatio Gates Spafford, *A Gazetteer of the State of New York* (Albany: B. D. Packard, 1824).

9. Dwight H. Bruce, *Memorial History of Syracuse* (Syracuse: H. P. Smith, 1891), pp. 44, 71, 104-105, 130; Spafford, *Gazetteer* (1824), pp. 461-462; Shaw, *Erie Water West*, p. 243; Charles H. Cooley, *The Theory of Transportation* in *Publications of the American Economic Association*, IX (Baltimore: American Economic Association, 1894), pp. 90-100; *New York Assembly Journal* (1825), pp. 634-635; Benjamin DeWitt, *Memoir on the Onondaga Salt Springs and Salt Manufactories in the Western Part of the State of New York*...(Albany: Loring Andrews, 1798), pp. 5, 20-21; and Richard L. Ehrlich, "The Development of Manufacturing in Selected Counties in the Erie Canal Corridor, 1815-1860" (Ph.D. dissertation, State University of New York at Buffalo, 1972), pp. 169-170. Draining a swamp was not uncommon in early nineteenth century frontier settlements; see Blake McKelvey, *Rochester, The Water-Power City 1812-1855* (Cambridge: Harvard University Press, 1945), p. 66.

10. Bruce, *Onondaga's Centennial*, I, pp. 223-225; Harry N. Scheiber, *Ohio Canal Era: A Case Study of Government and the Economy, 1820-1861* (Athens: Ohio University Press, 1969), pp. 187-189; Harvey H. Segal,

"Canals and Economic Development," in Carter Goodrich, ed., *Canals and American Economic Development* (Port Washington, N.Y.: Kennikat Press, 1961; reissued, 1972), pp. 226-235.

11. Clark, *Onondaga*, II, pp. 166, 328-330; Bruce, *Memorial History of Syracuse*, p. 67; Spafford, *Gazetteer* (1813); Spafford, *Gazetteer* (1824); John W. Barber, *Historical Collections of the State of New York* (New York: Clark, Austin and Co., 1851), p. 252; Thurlow Weed, *Life of Thurlow Weed, including his Autobiography and a Memoir*, I (Boston: Houghton, Mifflin and Company, 1884), p. 90.

12. Zerah Hawley, *A Journey of a Tour Through Connecticut, Massachusetts, New York*...(New Haven: S. Converse, 1822), p. 117; Henry C. VanSchaack, *A History of Manlius Village* (Fayetteville, N.Y.: The Recorder Office, 1873), pp. 10-16; Weed, *Autobiography*, I, pp. 85-96 and II, pp. 13-15; letter from Azariah Smith, Manlius, New York, to his father, Middlefield, Massachusetts, February 9, 1830, reprinted in Albert V. House, Jr., "Two Yankee Traders in New York: Letters on the Financing of Frontier Merchants, 1808-1830," *New England Quarterly*, II (1938), 607-631.

13. Among the feeder canals proposed were the following: from Camillus to Onondaga Lake; from Onondaga Valley to the Chanango River; from Salina to the Susquehanna; from Brewerton to Syracuse; from Syracuse to Auburn; from Skaneateles Lake to the Erie Canal; and from Onondaga Hollow to Syracuse. In addition, there was agitation for canals from Manlius to Cortland Village, in neighboring Cortland County, and from Salina to Port Watson, located near Cortland Village. See also Bruce, *Onondaga's Centennial*, I, pp. 224-227; *Onondaga Gazette*, August 27, 1823; J. H. French, *Gazetteer of the State of New York*...(Syracuse: R. P. Smith, 1860), pp. 58-63; VanSchaak, *History of Manlius Village*, pp. 12-13; letter from Joseph Smith, Manlius, New York, to his brother, Middlefield, Massachusetts, November 24, 1825, in House, "Two Yankee Traders," p. 630.

14. Spafford, *Gazetteer* (1824), p. 114; Clark, *History of Onondaga*, II, p. 188; William A. Bird, "New York State Early Transportation," *Publications of the Buffalo Historical Society*, II (Buffalo: Bigelow Brothers, 1880), pp. 24-25; Louis Dow Scisco, *Early History of the Town of Van Buren, Onondaga County, New York* (Baldwinsville, N.Y.: W. F. Morris Publishing Company, 1895), pp. 22-29.

15. The crude rate of natural increase is calculated by the formula $\left(\frac{B - D}{P}\right)k$, where B is the total number of births during the year, D is the total number of deaths, P is the total population at the time of the census,

and k is 100. In Onondaga County this crude rate of natural increase in 1825 was 27.9 per thousand or 2.79 percent. If the assumption is made that the rate of natural increase in 1825 was the same as that for five years before and after the census year, this rate can be extended to the entire decade of the 1820s. The growth in population from natural increase alone for the ten-year period would have been 31.55 percent of the population in 1820. Since the total population change in the county was 42.2 percent for the decade, we can assume that 10.6 percent of this increase was due to the excess of the in-migration over out-migration. Admittedly, these figures are artificial. The crude rate of natural increase is based upon the total number of births and deaths in the county for 1825, both of which are undoubtedly incorrect. Moreover, it also assumes that the county had a closed population that year with no in- or out-migration, a situation clearly not true for Onondaga County. Since the census was taken within a period of a few months, however, the distortions to the crude rate of natural increase introduced by migration were probably kept to a minimum. When this rate is extended to the entire decade, however, we make the unwarranted assumption that the rate of natural increase remained the same over the entire period, for we project the rate of natural increase for 1825, for example, to each year between 1820 and 1829 and calculate the total percentage increase. In fact, the crude rate of natural increase for 1820 was probably different from that of 1825, and the transition between the two rates a gradual process. Despite these difficulties, however, the measure can be useful as an estimate for comparative purposes. Data are taken from the 1825 census of New York.

16. As Syracuse grew larger, the crude rate of natural increase in the city rose above that in the rural and village hinterland. This was a common pattern in the nineteenth century. See Adna Weber, *The Growth of Cities in the Nineteenth Century* (New York: Macmillan, 1899), pp. 333-334. Data are from the 1835 census of the state of New York. For a discussion of the declining rural birth rate, see Wendall H. Bash, "Differential Fertility in Madison County, New York, 1865," *Milbank Memorial Fund Quarterly*, 33 (1955), 161-186; and Richard A. Easterlin, "Population Change and Farm Settlement in the Northern United States," *Journal of Economic History,* 36 (1976), 45-75.

17. See Whitney R. Cross, *The Burned-Over District: The Social and Intellectual History of Enthusiastic Religion in Western New York, 1800-1850* (Ithaca: Cornell University Press, 1950), pp. 62-66; and Easterlin, "Population Change and Farm Settlement in the Northern United States."

18. See Spafford, *Gazetteer* (1824); and Thomas F. Gordon, *Gazetteer of the State of New York* (Philadelphia: privately printed, 1836), pp. 577-586.

19. "Town of Manlius and Vicinity" (typescript, Syracuse Public Library—probably written by Joseph Smith, a resident and census enumerator, in the 1840s).

20. One forwarding agent in 1829 offered to sell property "either east, west or north by the Canal, Lake, or River." However the certainty of the New York market was such that he was prepared to "make liberal advances on all produce destined to the New York market." See the *Onondaga Register and Syracuse Gazette*, December 23, 1829. Also, *Syracuse Advertiser,* March 15, 1826; *The Constitutionalist,* August 6, 1833; *The Western Business Directory* (New York: J. Doggett, Jr., [1840-1843]); and Gordon, *Gazetteer*, 582-584. For a general discussion of transportation and the nature of interregional trade, see Allan R. Pred, *Urban Growth and the Circulation of Information: The United States System of Cities, 1790-1840* (Cambridge: Harvard University Press, 1973), pp. 104-109. In addition, see Glenn Porter and Harold C. Livesay, *Merchants and Manufacturers: Studies in the Changing Structure of Nineteenth-Century Marketing* (Baltimore: Johns Hopkins University Press, 1971); Clarence H. Danhof, *Change in Agriculture: The Northern United States, 1820-1870* (Cambridge: Harvard University Press, 1969), pp. 27-48; and Carol Halpert Schwartz, "Retail Trade Development in New York State in the Nineteenth Century with Special Reference to the Country Store" (Ph.D. dissertation, Columbia University, 1963), pp. 5-10.

21. Spafford, *Gazetteer* (1824); and New York State Census, 1825, 1835.

22. *American Railroad Journal*, 18 (January 23, 1845), 58, quoting the *Journal* for 1840; and Danhof, *Change in Agriculture,* pp. 14-15, 45.

23. Willis Gaylord, "Agriculture of Onondaga County," *Transactions of the New York State Agricultural Society,* II (Albany: E. Mack, 1842), pp. 174-186; III (1843), pp. 546-549; George Geddes, *Report on the Agriculture and Industry of the County of Onondaga, State of New York* (Albany: Charles Van Benthuysen, 1860), pp. 105-110; Russell H. Anderson, "New York Agriculture Meets the West, 1830-1850," *Wisconsin Magazine of History*, 16 (1932-1933), 163-198; Harvey S. Perloff, et al., *Regions, Resources, and Economic Growth*, Resources for the Future, Inc. (Baltimore: Johns Hopkins University Press, 1960), pp. 199-200; and Spafford, *Gazetteer* (1824), p. 390.

24. *The* [*Syracuse*] *Constitutionalist,* October 23, 1833; Gordon, *Gazetteer*, p. 51; Thomas Senior Berry, *Western Prices Before 1861: A Study of the Cincinnati Market* (Cambridge: Harvard University Press, 1943), pp. 286-296; and Bruce, *Memorial History of Syracuse*, p. 400. Figures on salt production can be found in Clayton, *History of Onondaga County,* p. 54; and Ehrlich, "The Development of Manufacturing in Selected Counties in the Erie Canal Corridor, 1815-1860," p. 199.

25. Miller, *Enterprise of a Free People,* pp. 125-126, 146-149, 185-186.

26. *American Railroad Journal*, 5 (February 13, 1836), 85; Scisco, *Early History of Van Buren*, pp. 32-33; Bruce, *Memorial History of Syracuse*, pp. 90, 388; Clark, *Onondaga,* II, pp. 188-191; Bruce, *Onondaga's Centennial,* p. 952; and Geddes, *Report on Agriculture and Industry*, p. 82.

27. Report to the Canal Commissioners, *New York Assembly Documents*, 4 (1836), Document #261, 3-4; Clark, *Onondaga*, II, pp. 61-65, 235; Bruce, *Memorial History of Syracuse,* pp. 702-703; *Transactions of the New York State Agricultural Society*, 1842, pp. 366-370, and 1846, pp. 586-587; and *Onondaga Standard*, August 3, 1836.

28. New York State Census, 1825, 1835, 1845; Danhof, *Change in Agriculture*, pp. 31-32; Robert G. Albion, *The Rise of New York Port, 1815-1860* (New York: Charles Scribner's Sons, 1939), p. 89; Edward Hazen, *The Panorama of Professions and Trades; or Every Man's Book* (Philadelphia: Uriah Hunt, 1836), pp. 25-26; and Scheiber, *Ohio Canal Era*, pp. 200-203.

29. Gordon, *Gazetteer,* p. 579; New York State Census, 1825, 1835, 1845; and Victor S. Clark, *History of Manufactures in the United States,* I (Washington: Carnegie Institution of Washington, 1929), pp. 315-317.

30. There were some locally produced textiles as well. As early as 1822, a storekeeper in Onondaga Hollow purchased cotton for retailing from a textile factory in nearby Otsego County, and in the 1820s the Asa Eastwood family could purchase cotton more cheaply in Manlius than in New York City. Cotton factories were, however, usually located on or near good transportation facilities by the 1830s. See Rolla Milton Tryon, *Household Manufactures in the United States 1640-1860: A Study in Industrial History* (Chicago: University of Chicago Press, 1917); New York State Census, 1825, 1835; invoice book of Oren Tyler, Onondaga Hollow, 1822-1832, Onondaga Historical Association; and Asa Eastwood Papers, George Arents Research Library, Syracuse University.

31. For a discussion of the growth of manufacturing activity in urban areas in the 1830s, see Allan R. Pred, "Manufacturing in the American Mercantile City," in *The Spacial Dynamics of U.S. Urban-Industrial Growth, 1800-1914: Interpretive and Theoretical Essays* (Cambridge: M.I.T. Press, 1966), pp. 143-215; and Eric E. Lampard, "The History of Cities in the Economically Advanced Areas," *Economic Development and Cultural Change,* 3 (1955), 81-136.

32. Gordon, *Gazetteer,* pp. 577-586.

33. Lampard, "The History of Cities," 86-92; and Pred, "Manufacturing in the American Mercantile City."

34. See Roger L. Ransom, "Interregional Canals and Economic Specialization in the Antebellum United States," *Explorations in Entrepreneurial History,* 2nd Ser., 5 (1967), 12-35; Albert W. Niemi, Jr., "A

Further Look at Interregional Canals and Economic Specialization, 1820-1840,'' *Explorations in Entrepreneurial History*, 2nd Ser., 7 (1970), 499-520; and Ransom, ''A Closer Look at Canals and Western Manufacturing,'' *Explorations in Entrepreneurial History*, 2nd Ser., 8 (1971), 501-508.

35. Gordon, *Gazetteer,* pp. 577-586.

CHAPTER 4

Transportation Innovation and Urban Growth: The Railroad

Between 1840 and 1860, a second major transportation innovation in Onondaga County—the railroad—intensified the social and economic changes set in motion after the construction of the Erie Canal. Unlike the canal, the railroad did not directly interrupt established development patterns nor alter the distribution of population in the county (except in the southern part of Onondaga where there had been no canals) nor did it disturb the existing relationships between cities and smaller settlements. Although technologically a transportation innovation, the railroad operated within a previously established transportation context in Onondaga County. The first county railroads were built as feeders to the canal system, and in time, interregional railroads were constructed between cities along earlier traffic routes. Instead of introducing new traffic and marketing patterns or stimulating the growth of new population centers, railroads in the canal counties tended to reinforce the effect of earlier transportation changes.[1]

The most important effect of the construction of the rail network was to solidify the position of Syracuse as a key transportation center in central New York. The rail lines that came into the city augmented existing canals and highways both for regional and interregional traffic and commerce. As a result, the city's role as a regional commercial center was enhanced, and the city's population continued to expand. During this period the two settlements of Syracuse and Salina were combined into the larger, Syracuse, which dominated the county hinterland more fully than ever before.

Population and agricultural changes that had begun in the hinterland during the canal period continued during the years of railway expansion. Neither the rural population decline nor the process of population coalescence into hinterland villages abated. As the railroad opened alternative markets for Onondaga farmers in the 1840s and 1850s, western competition with Onondaga agricultural products grew more intense. The railroads offered Onondaga farmers a competitive advantage over farmers in the Great Lakes region by providing them with fast transportation to eastern markets for perishable foodstuffs. Perhaps of greater significance, the railroad-related growth of Syracuse created a local urban market for county produce which replaced Onondaga's dwindling share of the national grain market.

Less important than agricultural changes were industrial changes in the county in this period. Most industrial firms continued to be locally oriented, although Syracuse, with its central location and regional marketing capabilities, supported a more varied range of industrial activities than the hinterland. During the years from 1840 to 1860, the amount of capital invested in industry rose in both city and hinterland, but profits rose more quickly in Syracuse than in the rest of the county.

The possibility of railroad construction was first mentioned in Onondaga County shortly after construction of the Erie Canal. As early as 1826, the New York State Legislature granted a charter for a railroad from Syracuse to Binghamton, New York, connecting the southern counties with the Erie Canal and providing low-cost transportation via canal to the New York City market. Although the road proved too expensive to build at that time, the idea took hold that railroads as well as canals could be used as feeders to the Erie Canal system. By 1830, residents of Manlius Village, who had been trying for a number of years to get a feeder waterway to connect their village with the Erie Canal, began to think instead in terms of a rail connection with the canal. Unfortunately, their efforts on behalf of the railroad fared as poorly as had their ill-fated canal activities, and the road was never built.[2]

Railroad promoters did not limit their ambitions to the use of railroads as feeders to the canals; they also argued that the railroad would eventually replace the canal itself. Supporters of the railroads cited the speed, flexibility, and the relatively inexpensive construction of railroad beds against the great time and expense required to construct a canal. Canals could only be built on fairly level terrain, they further maintained, whereas railroad tracks could be laid on both mountainous and flat land. Moreover, while the canal was forced to close for approximately five months each winter when its water was frozen, the railroad could operate throughout the year.[3]

Despite the opposition of canal supporters who claimed that canal transportation was far cheaper than rail transportation, particularly for heavy and bulky goods, a railroad between Auburn and Syracuse was chartered in 1834. Although many of the railroad's proponents argued that it would supplant the canal system, this first railroad in Onondaga County was planned only as a feeder, running the twenty-five miles from the village of Auburn, in Cayuga County west of Skaneateles, northeast to the Erie Canal at Syracuse. (See Figure 7.) Primarily interested in more efficient access to the Erie Canal, the railroad's supporters argued that the line would be profitable if 10,000 tons of goods were transported annually between Auburn and the canal at Syracuse. The proprietor of the local stagecoach line further maintained that the average of sixty people who traveled each day between the two cities were all potential rail passengers.

As was the case with supporters of the projected feeder canals, backers of the feeder railroads were largely residents of settlements off the canal—in this case, Auburn. In fact, most of the 4,000 shares of stock in the new railroad were sold to residents of Auburn. In addition to coveting a closer connection with the canal at Syracuse, stockholders hoped to draw business from the southern part of the state through Auburn to the canal at Syracuse. Some were even considering creating a combined canal-railroad connec-

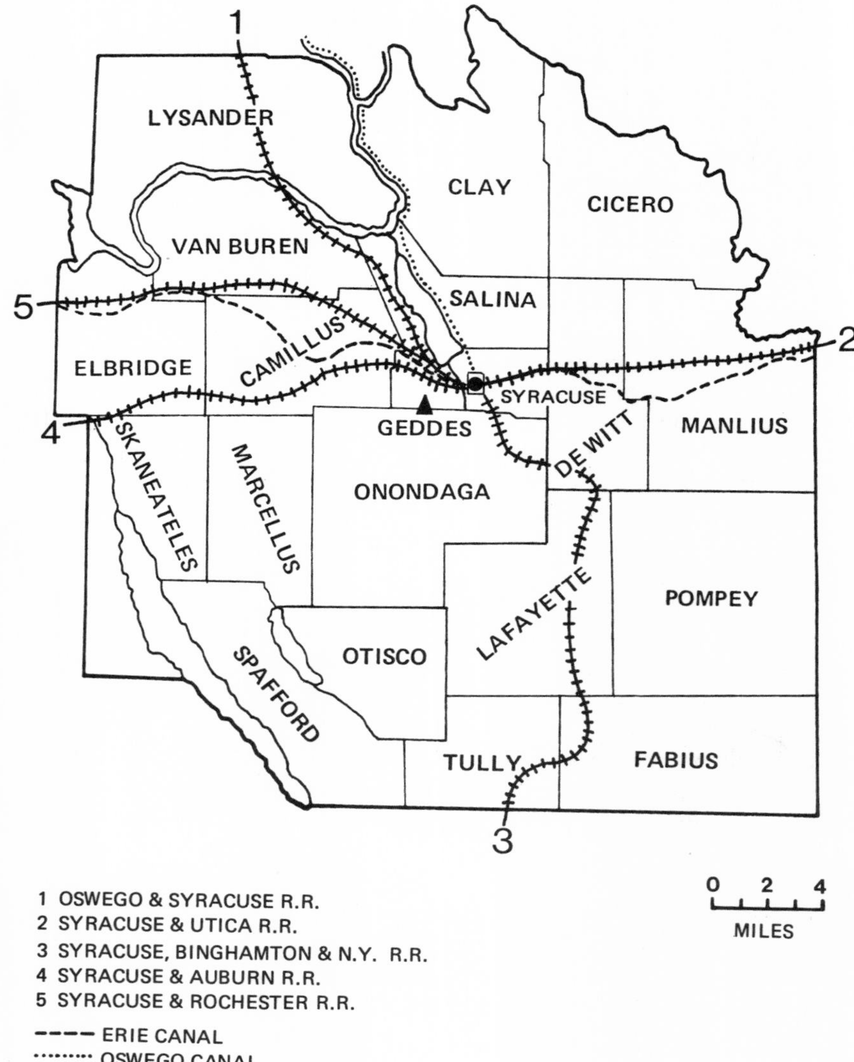

Figure 7. Railroads in Onondaga County, 1855

tion with Syracuse by building a canal between Auburn and Oswaco Lake. It was also hoped that eventually the railroad would become part of a rail line across New York.[4]

Despite these dreams, the impact of Auburn and Syracuse Railroad was in reality quite modest. While the road was generally welcomed, it faced competition from both the stagecoach and the canal. The stage line proved less serious a threat than the canal since its organization and its supporters' political power were local rather than statewide. For example, J. M. Sherwood, a government mail contractor as well as manager of a stagecoach line in Auburn, contracted to operate the railroad, keeping half the receipts from freight and passengers in return. By contracting with Sherwood, the railroad company succeeded in capturing the mail contract and eliminating stage competition at the same time. Canal interests were more powerful than the stagecoach interests and thus more difficult to combat. Canal supporters understood that although the Auburn and Syracuse Railroad was primarily designed to function as a feeder to the canal, its track gauge would fit into a railroad line crossing the state from the Hudson River to Buffalo, roughly along the same route as the Erie Canal. Consequently canal interests in the state legislature secured a stipulation in the railroad's charter that the company would pay the Commissioners of the Canal Fund the equivalent of canal tolls on all property, with the exception of passengers' baggage, that the railroad transported. In 1838 this requirement was modified to apply only in those months the canal was in use. These provisions or modification of them were applied to all east-west railroads along the canal and were not lifted until 1851.[5]

Many local railroads were incorporated in the late 1830s and the 1840s but, unlike the Auburn and Syracuse, were never built. The only local railroads constructed as planned were the Syracuse and Onondaga Railroad and the Skaneateles Railroad. Opened in 1836, the Syracuse and Onondaga connected the stone quarries in Onondaga Hollow with Syracuse and the Erie Canal, a distance of several miles. Since stone from these quarries was used extensively in canal construction, easy access to the quarries was important for the enlargement of the Erie Canal, which had been approved by the state legislature in 1835. The Skaneateles Railroad began operating in 1840 and led from the village of Skaneateles, located at the head of Skaneateles Lake near the western border of the county, to a junction on the Auburn and Syracuse Railroad. Not an economic success, the railroad was closed in 1850, and replaced by a plank road; its passenger business went to a stagecoach line. Other chartered railroads—the Syracuse Stone Railroad, the Brewerton and Syracuse Railroad, and the railroad from Salina to Fort Watson—were never constructed.[6]

In addition to railroads, local transportation was eased by the construction of plank roads. Onondaga County participated in the plank road craze or fever that swept the nation in the late 1840s and the 1850s, and the first plank road in the United States was built from Salina to Central Square, Oswego County, in 1847. Seven additional plank roads leading to Syracuse were built by 1851. Although the Syracuse and Oswego Plank Road ran thirty-two miles, all the other new roads were between eight and eighteen miles long and were intended primarily for local traffic. In addition to providing a relatively smooth ride, these roads were cheap and easy to build, consisting of wooden planks laid across two parallel stringers. Unfortunately they were also expensive to maintain and because of maintenance costs rarely repaid the investors. The result was rapid deterioration of the roads after a few years' use. Temporarily, however, they facilitated local access to Syracuse and further encouraged hinterland visits to the city.[7]

As important to the growth of Syracuse as local transportation improvements were the railroads connecting Syracuse with other major cities in central New York. The Syracuse and Utica Railroad was opened in 1839, the Oswego and Syracuse in 1848, and the Syracuse and Rochester in 1853. All three railroads cut through territory already served by the canal system. In 1853, the New York Central Railroad was formed by a merger of the lateral east-west railroads of New York. Including the Auburn and Syracuse Railroad, the Syracuse and Utica, and the Syracuse and Rochester, the New York Central established a single rail network that followed the route of the Erie Canal.

A fourth interregional railroad, the Syracuse and Binghamton, finally opened a direct transportation connection between the southern counties and the Erie Canal at Syracuse in 1854. As mentioned earlier, the railroad had been first proposed in 1826. Chartered and rechartered a number of times afterward, it received little support in Syracuse where railroads which could tap larger markets were more easily subscribed.[8]

Because the railroads, with one exception, followed the transportation routes of the canals, they had considerably less impact upon Onondaga County than had the Erie Canal, simply providing a faster alternative form of transportation without immediately opening up new markets. In addition, the railroads were initially unable to compete with the canals in transporting heavy goods since with iron rather than steel rails and wheels, the first railroads could carry only a limited amount of weight. Rail competition in carrying property was further hampered by the provisions in railroad charters for collecting canal tolls on all goods transported by rail. Thus canals remained the most important means of transporting freight prior to 1850.[9]

The Syracuse and Binghamton Railroad was the exception to this pattern. Because it passed through townships in the southern part of the county that were located off the canals and dependent on inefficient turnpikes for interregional transportation, the Syracuse and Binghamton caused more immediate changes in Onondaga County than other railroads built in these years. The influence of the Syracuse and Binghamton upon turnpike villages in southern townships was similar to the earlier influence of the Erie Canal upon the villages in central and northern Onondaga County. For example, Summit Station, a stop on the Syracuse and Binghamton line, became an important market for farmers in Tully and Fabius townships. Its growth, however, caused the decline of the turnpike villages of Fabius and Apulia, which had previously enjoyed that trade. In addition, the rail station of LaFayette, a mile east of the village of LaFayette, attracted the trade of both Cardiff and LaFayette, bringing an end to the growth of the two turnpike villages.[10]

In addition to luring trade from turnpike villages to railroad stations in southern townships, other newly constructed railroads captured passenger traffic from the stagecoaches throughout the county and forced the remaining stagecoach lines out of business. Passengers deserted the stages for the railroads because of the smoother and faster ride the railroads gave. Even the mail contracts went over to the railroads as soon as they were built, as we have seen in the case of the Auburn and Syracuse Railroad. Turnpike inns lost their customers and stagecoach drivers lost their jobs. For example, the railroad destroyed the business of several stagecoach lines going through the village of Manlius, while the village of Marcellus completely lost its stage line with the opening of the Auburn and Syracuse Railroad. As a result, both villages experienced economic hardship during the ensuing years.[11]

However, more important than the economic difficulties of certain hinterland villages was the effect of the railroads on Syracuse. Regardless of the original reasons for building the railroads, the major impact of their construction was to solidify the position of Syracuse as a leading transportation center in central New York. As early as 1839, after only two railroads had been built, Syracuse was hailed in a national journal as an "enterprising, enlightened village. . .destined to become a great inland city." By 1854, railroads came into Syracuse from four directions, connecting the city with Lake Ontario in the north and the Pennsylvania coal fields in the south as well as with cities on the Hudson River and the Great Lakes. As the city's transportation facilities expanded, its population more than quadrupled from 6,256 in 1840 to 28,119 in 1860, a growth of 350 percent over two decades. This rapid growth was accompanied by a new legal status in 1848 when the villages of Syracuse and Salina were incorporated together as the city of Syracuse.[12]

Syracuse steadily played a more important role in the daily lives of hinterland residents as it came to dominate the county's economy through its expanded commercial and transportation facilities. Hinterland residents who had been going to Syracuse for years to take care of legal matters increasingly turned to the canal city for other reasons as well. As it grew, Syracuse frequently replaced the small- and medium-sized county villages as the primary social and commercial center for hinterland residents. Political meetings, agricultural fairs, and even meetings of the Onondaga Agricultural Society were held in Syracuse rather than in the hinterland.

Illustrative of the changing orientation toward Syracuse among hinterland residents were the experiences of Asa Eastwood and

William B. Harris. Eastwood, a farmer and businessman who emigrated from New York City to Cicero in the northeastern corner of the county in 1817, traded in the villages of Manlius, Orville, and Salina throughout the 1820s. He even opened a store and manufactured salt for a time in Salina. However in the 1830s, he began to go to Syracuse more often than to the smaller hinterland towns he had frequented in the 1820s, and he regularly began to record Syracuse prices in his diaries. In the winter he brought wood in sleighs to the city where he sold it at the salt works, and in the summer he sold fruit in Syracuse. In the 1840s and the 1850s, Eastwood periodically went to the city for social visits. Gradually he began to make all of his purchases in Syracuse, including the purchase of wholesale goods for his Cicero store, which he had previously supplied directly from New York City and Utica. By the 1850s, Eastwood and his wife were traveling to Syracuse almost weekly for meetings of the agricultural society, for visits with friends, or simply for shopping.[13]

Another visitor to Syracuse was William B. Harris, who bought a farm in rural Cicero in 1837. According to his diary, he went into Syracuse fifty-four times over the course of two and one-half years. Most of these trips were made for business or legal reasons, yet the city's transportation facilities proved another important factor in bringing hinterland residents like Harris to the city. Nearly one in five trips Harris made to Syracuse involved meeting friends and relatives arriving by canal or railroad or bringing his guests and visitors to the city to continue their travels by rail or canal. In addition to these business and travel-related visits, Harris made his major purchases, including farm machinery, furniture, and clothing, in Syracuse. The trips to Syracuse made by Eastwood and Harris—and other hinterland residents like them—were a response to the expansion of transportation and commercial facilities in the city in the period of railroad construction. In turn, these customers from the hinterland further stimulated the city's economy and contributed to its growth through their purchases.[14]

In sharp contrast to the population growth in Syracuse, the population decline which had begun in the 1830s in the rural areas of the county continued during the years in which the railroad network expanded. While the railroad had no direct influence on out-migration by hinterland residents, it indirectly contributed to the decline of hinterland commercial and industrial facilities by encouraging the development of superior facilities in the regional transportation center, Syracuse. The railroad was also partially responsible for the rising price of land in the county, a factor which, coupled with the sagging market for Onondaga farm products in the 1830s and 1840s, discouraged the proliferation of small, owner-operated farms. While the transportation-related growth of Syracuse provided a local market for Onondaga farmers by the 1850s and thus revitalized the agricultural economy of the hinterland, the agricultural population of the hinterland was then considerably smaller than it had been in 1825.

Between 1840 and 1850, the total population of the hinterland increased only 5 percent. Given an estimated crude rate of natural increase for the decade of 21 percent in the hinterland, this low total population gain indicates that the net rate of out-migration was 17 percent of the 1840 population. The only significant growth in the county hinterland occurred in the northern and northeastern townships, which were settled later than the rest of the county and were comparatively underdeveloped in 1840. Of these townships, Lysander experienced the greatest population growth, due largely to the expansion of the village of Baldwinsville, and increased its population in the 1840s by 35 percent.[15] (See Figure 8.)

In the following decade, the population of the entire hinterland actually underwent an absolute decline overall of 3 percent. The largest growth in this period took place in the townships of Geddes and Salina, which bordered Syracuse, and in Elbridge, west of the city on both canal and rail routes.

As the total population of the hinterland stagnated, the proportion of its residents living in county villages continued to increase in the 1840s and the 1850s in every township except Skaneateles. These villages continued to offer commercial and industrial opportunities to new residents that the rural areas could not equal because of the growing tendency to restrict rural economic activities to agricultural pursuits. By 1855, 29 percent of the residents of the county hinterland lived in villages—almost twice as high a proportion as in 1836. The townships of Elbridge, Manlius, Geddes, and Salina all had more than 40 percent of their populations living in

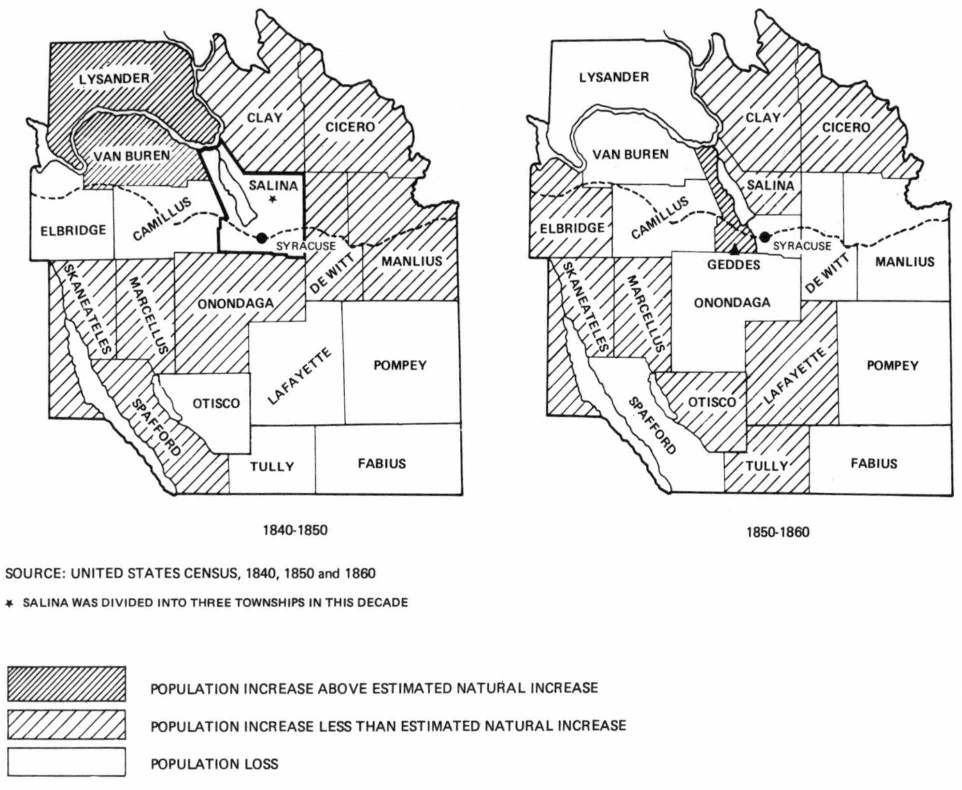

LYSANDER
VAN BUREN
CLAY
CICERO
SALINA ★
ELBRIDGE
CAMILLUS
SYRACUSE
DE WITT
MANLIUS
SKANEATELES
MARCELLUS
ONONDAGA
LAFAYETTE
POMPEY
OTISCO
SPAFFORD
TULLY
FABIUS
1840-1850
LYSANDER
VAN BUREN
CLAY
CICERO
SALINA
ELBRIDGE
CAMILLUS
SYRACUSE
GEDDES
DE WITT
MANLIUS
SKANEATELES
MARCELLUS
ONONDAGA
LAFAYETTE
POMPEY
OTISCO
SPAFFORD
TULLY
FABIUS
1850-1860
SOURCE: UNITED STATES CENSUS, 1840, 1850 and 1860
★ SALINA WAS DIVIDED INTO THREE TOWNSHIPS IN THIS DECADE
POPULATION INCREASE ABOVE ESTIMATED NATURAL INCREASE
POPULATION INCREASE LESS THAN ESTIMATED NATURAL INCREASE
POPULATION LOSS

villages, while Camillus, Lysander, and Skaneateles had over 30 percent. All the townships with large village populations had greater than average population growth during the twenty-year period because of village population growth. However, even townships that had been losing population were at the same time increasing the village component of the remaining population—a process of population coalescence that had been taking place since the late 1820s. In short, there was a continued exodus from the countryside in the 1840s and 1850s and a steady population growth in hinterland villages as well as in Syracuse itself. (See Figure 9.) Again, the only exception to the growth of hinterland villages in this period was in the area crossed by the Syracuse and Binghamton Railroad in 1854, where villages away from the rail lines suffered from the competition of the new railroad villages.[16]

The process of agricultural change in Onondaga County, like the decline in the growth of the hinterland population, continued unabated during the period of railroad construction and expansion. If the twenty years following the construction of the Erie Canal in Onondaga County saw a vast change in terms of agricultural access to interregional markets, the subsequent two decades were characterized by the growth of a substantial regional market within the county alongside a vastly altered national market for agricultural produce. In effect, the railroad provided some solutions to the farmers' dilemma. The speed of rail transportation opened new markets in eastern cities for perishable goods from Onondaga while the same transportation improvements contributed to the enlargement of a local urban market for county produce in Syracuse.

Responding to these markets, farmers in Onondaga County gradually changed the nature of local agriculture between 1840 and 1860. They began to diversify their crops to serve the local and distant urban markets as they also turned to exotic or speciality crops, such as tobacco and fruit, which were unlikely to inspire competition in the wheatlands to the west. Within the county there was a sectional response to the new market and agricultural conditions. In general, farmers in the southern part of the county concentrated on grazing and dairying, those in a broad semicircle from south to northeast around Syracuse increased their production of garden, orchard, and dairy products, and farmers northwest of Syracuse turned increasingly to tobacco culture. Much of the land

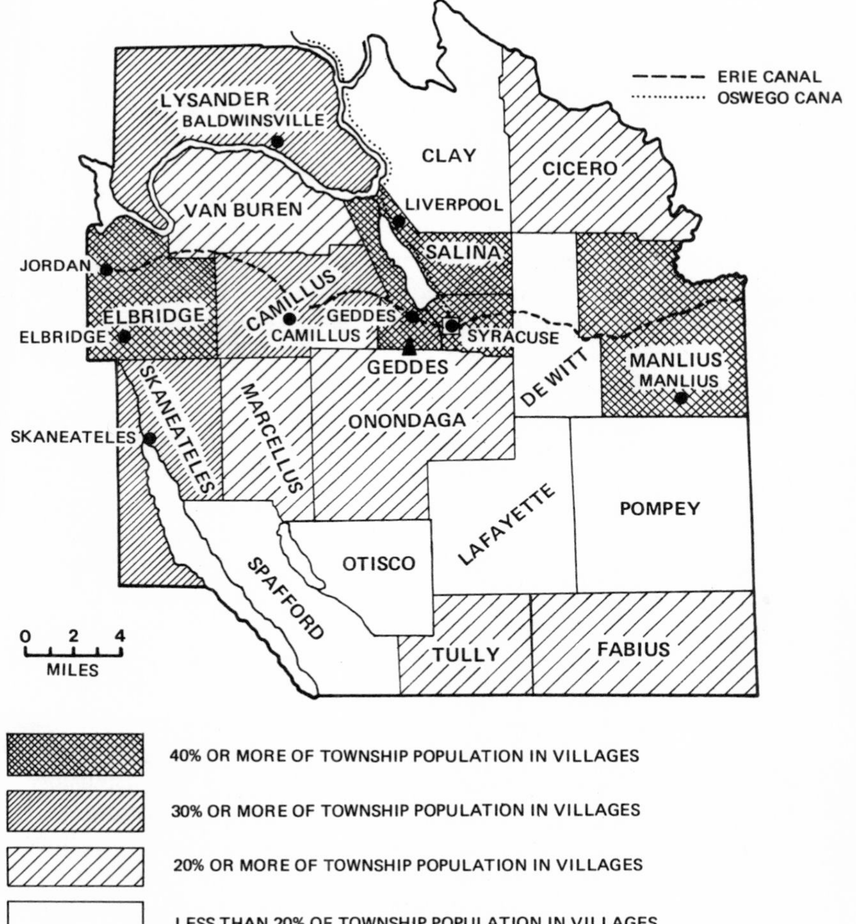

SOURCE: New York State Census, 1855, and French, *Gazetteer* (1860)

Figure 9. Percentage of Hinterland Population in Villages, 1855

previously planted in cash grains like wheat and barley was instead planted in corn and oats which could be used to feed livestock.

Further evidence of a countywide shift in agricultural patterns can be seen in the rise in the proportion of total improved farmland devoted to pasture and meadows.[17]

Despite farmers' response to the new markets opened up by the railroads, their decisions to change agricultural patterns were frequently impelled by necessity rather than choice. The declining wheat yields of the 1830s and the growing competition of western wheat were intensified in the 1840s. By mid-decade, soil exhaustion and insects also began to make inroads on wheat yields until by 1855, wheat production per acre in Onondaga County was only half the 1845 level. Although agricultural commentators blamed the low yields of 1854-55 on unusual crop failures due to poor growing conditions throughout the county, farmers had already responded to the reality of lower yields by cutting down their total wheat acreage nearly 50 percent between 1845 and 1855. Despite improvement in wheat yields after 1855, the proportion of farmland in the county planted in wheat declined still further between 1855 and 1865. Wheat farming for Onondaga farmers was simply no longer as profitable in comparison to other crops as it had been earlier.

Onondaga had been the leading barley producing county in the state in the 1830s, yet outside the southwestern portion of the county, barley, like wheat, became gradually less important to Onondaga agriculturists in the late 1840s and 1850s. Between 1855 and 1865, there was a countywide decline in acreage planted in barley. The reason for the shift away from barley was ostensibly the farmers' sympathies with the temperance movement resulting in their dislike of growing a crop which was used in the distilling process. In actuality, however, barley yields in Onondaga were cut in half by the depredations of insects. Declining barley yields, like declining wheat yields, encouraged farmers to turn to other crops.

Farmers in the southern townships concentrated their energies most heavily on cattle and other livestock because the soils of Pompey, LaFayette, Fabius, Tully, Otisco, Spafford, and parts of Marcellus were recognized as particularly well-suited to grazing. To accommodate growing herds, farms were larger in these townships than in the rest of the county. Moreover, the population of these grazing townships was declining faster than that of other townships in the hinterland, as might be expected in an area without major villages undergoing a shift to a less labor-intensive form of agricultural activity. Sheep raising, although generally of diminishing importance throughout the county after 1840, remained a significant part of the economies of the southern townships; farmers from other parts of the county who wanted to purchase sheep came to these townships to do so. Dairy farming, particularly the production of cheese and butter, was another important agricultural industry in the southern part of the county. Onondaga County began to export large amounts of cheese. In 1855, 527,770 pounds of cheese were produced in the townships of Fabius alone, almost two-thirds of the total amount of cheese made in the county, but by 1860 total cheese production in the county rose as foreign markets for cheese became more important and Fabius's share of total cheese production then fell to 59 percent. Milk was not an export from this region, since the southern townships were too far from Syracuse to make fresh milk sales profitable.[18]

In the 1840s and 1850s, farmers in central and northern Onondaga County turned increasingly to orchards and market gardening instead of grains in response to the growing urban markets. Long before white Americans had arrived in the area, Indians in what is now Onondaga County had orchards of apple and plum trees, many of which still produced fruit for their new owners well into the nineteenth century. As early as 1830, commercial nurseries, reportedly the first to be set up west of the Hudson River, were established in Syracuse. By the 1840s, local farmers considered orchards, particularly apple orchards, as a source of income as well as food for the household. When orchards were bearing fruit, the profit per acre was almost three times as great as the profit per acre of wheat. In 1850, the leading fruit-producing townships in the county were Onondaga and Pompey in the south and Lysander, Van Buren, Clay, and Cicero across the northern part of the county. Ten years later, the value of orchard produce had increased throughout the county, although Lysander and Onondaga continued to lead all other counties in the value of orchard produce. They were followed by DeWitt, located next to Syracuse, which increased the value of its orchard produce by 123 percent between 1850 and 1860.[19]

Farmers in the townships circling the city also began to plant more acres in garden crops to meet the growing needs of both the city of Syracuse and eastern urban markets in the late 1840s. During the decade of the 1850s, the value of market garden produce increased fourfold in the county. With virtually no market gardening in the western townships, production centered in the area south and east of Syracuse and occasionally reached north of the city. Over time, however, market gardening tended to be concentrated in the area immediately surrounding Syracuse and in the township of Onondaga, which had excellent sheltered land in the Onondaga Valley and easy access to Syracuse. By the 1860s, Onondaga township led all other townships in the county not only in the production of fruit but also in potatoes and market garden products. These crops were eagerly awaited in the city, and the daily newspaper noted with satisfaction the days each summer when the first cherries and strawberries from Onondaga were for sale in Syracuse stores.[20]

Another response to the decline of marketable grains was the growth of tobacco farming in the northwestern part of the county. Tobacco culture began in Marcellus in the 1840s and soon spread to Salina and, more important, to Lysander and Van Buren. By 1855, there were 471 acres planted in tobacco in the county, most of it in Marcellus, and 554,987 pounds of tobacco were harvested. Less than ten years later, in 1864, almost eight times as many acres were reserved for tobacco, with the center of tobacco culture firmly set in Lysander and Van Buren.

Other county farmers, who were not turning to fruit and vegetable culture, took advantage of transportation improvements introduced by the railroad to open up new markets for the products they previously sold only locally. By shipping perishables to eastern markets via the railroad, Onondaga County farmers successfully competed with agriculturists in the Great Lakes region. Products such as poultry, butter, and fresh meats, for example, were in demand in eastern cities and needed to be marketed more quickly than was possible on the long canal ride from Lake Erie to the eastern cities. These products could be shipped more rapidly to the East from Onondaga County by the new railroads than from the Great Lakes area by either railroad or canal.[21]

As farmers turned away from marketable grains, agricultural activities in Onondaga County began to sort themselves out on a modified von Thünian basis for the first time in the development of the county hinterland. J.H. von Thünen suggested that agricultural activities were related to distance from the market or urban center. Intensive agriculture, generally market gardening, was practiced in the first concentric zone around the city, and successive zones were characterized by increasingly less intensive forms of agriculture. In Onondaga, market garden and orchard produce, for example, were heavily concentrated to the south and east of Syracuse. The result of this geographic tilt to the southeast in the market supply area of the city was that von Thünen zones of agricultural production did not arrange themselves neatly around Syracuse in concentric circles but rather in what were at best concentric ellipses. The proportion of land specifically devoted to particular crops cannot be determined within township boundaries without undertaking the prohibitively time-consuming and difficult job of reconstructing the landownership and land transfer patterns of each parcel in the county. Consequently, no exact lines of the limits of various types of horticulture and husbandry finer than township boundaries can be drawn. In general, however, very rough elliptical zones of market gardens, orchards, dairying both for milk and the more transportable cheese, and finally other grazing surrounded Syracuse in the city's Onondaga hinterland.[22]

Simultaneous with the shift in agricultural practices to accommodate local and highly specialized long distance markets was a reversal in the landholding trends of previous decades in the county hinterland. The average size of Onondaga farms had been growing larger for several decades until by 1850, the mean landholding in the county was 96.9 acres. Between 1850 and 1860, however, the average size of farms in the county declined by more than ten acres and the mean landholding was only 84.0 acres in 1860. For example, landholdings in the townships of Elbridge and Camillus grew from an average of 53.8 and 47.7 acres in 1825 to an average of 118.6 and 120.2 acres in 1850. By 1860, farms in the two townships averaged only 86.5 and 101.0 acres, respectively. (See Table 4.1.)

Table 4.1. **Land Values by Township, 1850-1860**

	Mean Value per Acre $		Cash Value per Farm $		Mean Size Landholding in Acres	
	1850	*1860*	*1850*	*1860*	*1850*	*1860*
Located on Erie Canal or east/west railroads:						
Manlius	41	61	3,485	4,777	85	79
DeWitt	51	77	3,571	5,901	70	77
Salina	49	77	4,346	5,941	88	77
Syracuse	40	173	5,760	12,549	145	73
Geddes	45	77	3,760	6,105	84	79
Camillus	42	68	5,639	6,849	120	101
Elbridge	47	71	4,945	6,102	119	87
VanBuren	51	70	4,281	6,134	83	88
Skaneateles	44	47	4,988	4,212	115	75
Mean	46	80	4,531	6,508	101	82
Mean (excl. Syracuse)	46	69	4,377	5,753	96	83
Not located on Erie Canal or east/west railroads:						
Cicero	34	56	2,190	3,465	65	74
Clay	38	51	2,645	3,308	70	65
Lysander	35	50	3,253	4,341	93	87
Pompey	34	49	3,509	4,485	101	93
LaFayette	35	46	3,294	3,971	93	86
Fabius	28	41	3,281	4,971	118	120
Tully	29	40	3,202	4,101	111	101
Otisco	28	43	2,717	3,732	98	87
Spafford	30	39	2,731	3,342	92	86
Marcellus	38	54	3,498	3,647	91	68
Onondaga	43	56	4,204	4,319	97	77
Mean	34	48	3,138	3,971	94	86

Source: Manuscript Schedules, United States Census of Agriculture, 1850 and 1860.

The reason for the decline in farm size was the continued rise in land prices, which increased by nearly 50 percent over the decade. In 1850, the value per acre of farmland in the county averaged $39 (including both improved and unimproved land). By 1860, the mean value of farmland in the county had risen to $62, if the expensive land in Syracuse township is included, and $57 if the Syracuse farmland is excluded from the calculations. The effect of this rapid rise in land prices in the 1850s was to require a greater cash outlay from farmers purchasing land. This forced prospective landowners to buy smaller parcels of land and priced many other farmers out of the land market completely.[23]

The increase in land values in Onondaga between 1850 and 1860 was due both to the general inflation in land values and to the growth of Syracuse and the market advantages of the canal and railroads. Land located on the Erie Canal and the railroads was more valuable than land not so fortuitously located. In addition, the value of farmland declined with distance from Syracuse. If, for example, a line were drawn from Syracuse to the edge of the county in any direction, land values by township could be seen to decline along the line away from Syracuse. (See Figure 10.) Moreover, lines drawn to the east or west of Syracuse would go through areas of higher land values than lines drawn to the north or south of the city, because land values were higher along the transportation routes.[24]

The continuation of the agricultural trends of the 1830s into the 1840s and 1850s was echoed in the continuation of earlier industrial trends during the period of railroad construction. Yet changes in the location and organization of industrial production were less sweeping than the agricultural changes taking place at the same time. The effect of industrial change on the development of city and hinterland—and on the populations of both areas—was consequently also less dramatic. The tendency observed earlier for new industries to form in the city and the larger hinterland villages rather than in rural areas continued, and the basic orientation of county industrial activity—outside of the salt industry and possibly the production of ready-to-wear clothing—remained local. Unlike agricultural production, manufacturing in both city and hinterland existed largely to fill county needs rather than those of distant markets, and thus the pattern of industrial production changed slowly.[25]

Seven industries in the county employed 200 or more workers in 1860 and together their employees comprised nearly 61 percent of

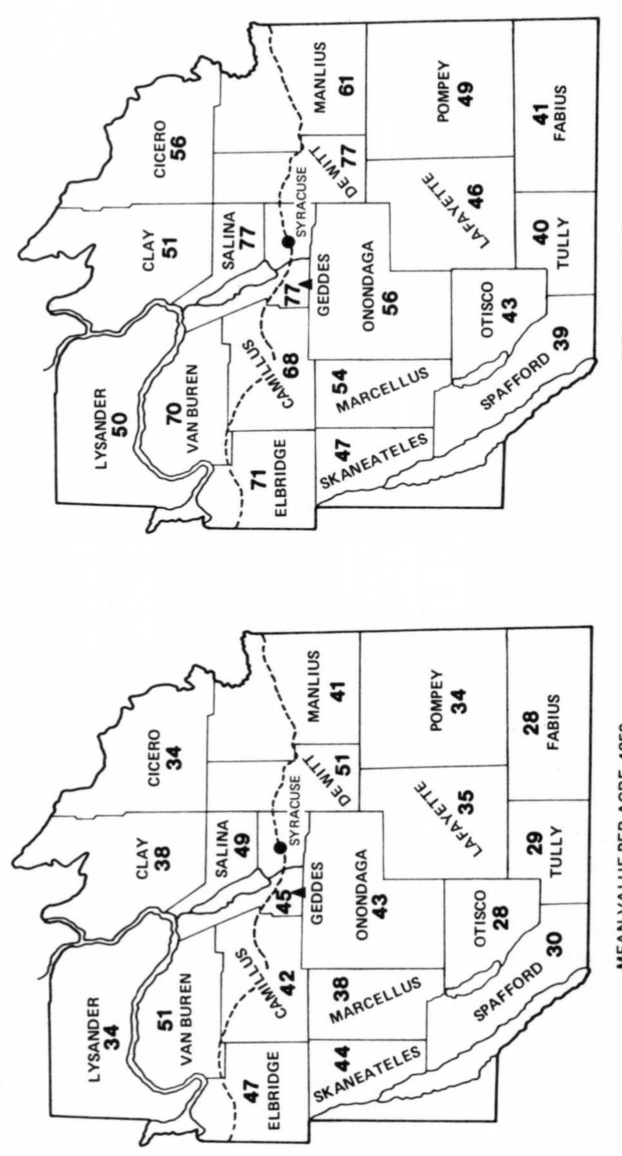

SOURCE: MANUSCRIPT SCHEDULES, U.S. CENSUS OF AGRICULTURE, 1850 and 1860

Figure 10. Value of Land in Onondaga County, 1850 and 1860 (in dollars)

the industrial work force in the county. The salt industry remained the leading industry in the county between 1840 and 1860. A second important area of manufacture in Onondaga was the production of barrels for shipping the salt, five-sixths of which went out of the state of New York. Other large industries in the county included the construction of boots and shoes, ready-to-wear apparel, and woolen goods. A sizable proportion of the county's industrial employees were engaged in the production of carriages, wagons, and sleighs, and with the expansion of tobacco culture in the county, cigar making became increasingly important.[26]

Although all of these industries were found in both the city of Syracuse and its hinterland, there were observable differences between industrial production in the two areas. Syracuse had both larger and more varied industries than the hinterland because it had more capital for investment, a larger work force, and better commercial facilities. The growth of the city's population between 1840 and 1860 and the rise in the number of hinterland residents who shopped in Syracuse also provided more potential customers for the products of industry in Syracuse than in the smaller towns of the hinterland. Certain industrial activities—such as cigar making or the manufacture of tableware and pianofortes—were too esoteric or specialized for hinterland manufacture. These industries required the skilled employees and commercial advantages that the growing regional and transportation center of Syracuse could provide. Other industrial firms, such as boot and shoe factories, hardware factories, and machine shops, were found in both the city and the hinterland villages but were considerably larger in the city. For example, in Syracuse in 1855 there were three tailor shops employing a total of 250 people, while the three largest tailor shops in the hinterland together employed only forty-three people. Overall, there was an average of 8.5 employees per firm in Syracuse in 1860, but if only the firms outside the city's salt-making wards (wards one and two) are considered, the average number of employees per firm rises to 21.9. At this time the average number of employees per firm in the hinterland was 4.3.[27]

Between 1850 and 1860, the total number of industrial firms decreased in both city and hinterland. At the same time, the capital invested in industry and the value of raw materials used in manufacturing rose in both areas. In Syracuse, the average value of the products of industry increased 86 percent per firm while for the hinterland the mean value of the products of industry rose an average of 34 percent per firm. In short, the decrease in the total number of industrial firms in both Syracuse and the county hinterland meant that each remaining firm was more heavily capitalized, expended more on an average for raw materials, and earned more on the sale of its products, with the greatest profits accruing to urban industrial enterprises. The overall rise in the average number of workers per firm during the same decade suggests that a process of industrial consolidation and growth was taking place in both areas and that Syracuse, with the higher average level of employment per firm and greater growth in profits per firm over the decade, was experiencing more consolidation and industrial growth than the hinterland.[28]

The leading industrial employer in Syracuse and in the county as a whole was the salt industry which, together with the related cooperage industry, employed approximately 800 men in Syracuse alone—nearly one-third of the male industrial work force in the city in 1860. There were hundreds of salt manufacturers in the city with an average of just over three employees per firm. Yet the impact of the salt industry on the economy of Syracuse was less than might be suggested by either the number of firms engaged in salt production or the number of individuals employed by those firms. In part, this was because the work was usually seasonal—with most salt production taking place in a seven-month period each year—and in part because the wages paid to salt boilers were generally lower than those paid for other types of work in the city. Moreover, wages of salt boilers failed to keep pace with the nationwide rise in industrial wages between 1850 and 1860. Salt producers' lack of control over the market led to wide variation in the prices salt brought and to repeated attempts to control both production and marketing among salt makers in the 1850s. Foreign competition began to cut into the market for Onondaga salt in the late 1840s; in response, county salt makers increased production, and some manufacturers even kept their salt works operating throughout the winter in order to raise their profits. The result, as might have been expected, was a glut of Onondaga salt on the market, and in 1850 salt could only be sold at a price below the actual cost of production. Attempts to organize salt producers failed because the industry was so decentralized. Despite the variability of the salt market, however, Onondaga salt production increased steadily through most of the 1850s.[29]

As befitted a transportation center, many Syracuse industries were directly dependent upon the transportation industries. These included boat building, coach and wagon construction, and one small iron rail manufacturing plant. Except for the latter, the manufacturing needs of the railroad industry were met in other cities because Syracuse did not have the necessary iron and coal to manufacture locomotives or large amounts of track. The most important of the transportation-related industries were the many small coach and wagon manufactories which produced conveyances for local rather than interregional transportation. The wagon and carriage industry was an exception to the general rule that urban industries were larger than hinterland industries, for more people were employed in wagon manufacture in the hinterland than in Syracuse, reflecting the greater demand in the hinterland for short-distance land transportation facilities.

By 1860, most hinterland industry was clustered in the villages, although one pocket of rural industry remained. Mottville, a small settlement with excellent water power facilities in the township of Skaneateles, had been an industrial settlement before the Erie Canal was built. Although its 1860 population was only 250, it boasted two machine shops, a chair factory, and a fork factory in addition to a foundry and a grist mill. The stability of this rural industrial enclave over a period when most rural industry was disappearing was undoubtedly due to its location on a good water power site only two miles north of the village of Skaneateles on the road to the village of Elbridge. However Mottville was atypical. Most hinterland manufacturing at this time took place in the larger villages such as Baldwinsville, located on the Seneca River in Lysander, and Fayetteville, a mile from the Erie Canal on a navigable feeder to the canal. This feeder—the Ledyard Canal—and the waters of Limestone Creek, which had been diverted to the settlement in 1848, provided water power to Fayetteville's industries. Hinterland manufacturing was also located in the villages of Jordan, Manlius, and Skaneateles.[30]

Industry in the Onondaga hinterland of the 1840s and the 1850s encompassed both the extraction of county mineral resources and residentiary processing and manufacturing industries similar to those dating from before the 1820s. In addition, new industries such as the manufacture of farm implements and wagons were formed to serve the evolving agricultural economy of the 1850s. The location of most hinterland industries reflected specific advantages of site rather than the commercial or transportation advantages which figured so importantly in the location of industry in the city. Plaster mills, stone cutting, and water lime manufacturing all had to be situated near the county's quarries. Moreover, industries which had been in the county since pre- and early canal days—the remaining distilleries, and grist and saw mills—generally manufactured or processed goods only for the immediate locality. They were usually located on the northern and southern edges of the county hinterland where the townships exhibited more varied industrial activities than townships closer to Syracuse and the urban market. Blacksmiths, tanners, harnessmakers, and shoemakers operated small businesses in these townships, rarely employing more than one person. These industries remained profitable wherever the distance from Syracuse was great enough to discourage urban competition for the household items they produced and where the local population was large enough to support the business.

In sum, the extension of an interregional railroad system through Onondaga County in the 1840s and the 1850s furthered but did not alter the earlier changes stimulated by the canals. As the city of Syracuse continued to grow, the hinterland population declined. County agriculture recovered in the 1850s as farmers turned from cash grain crops to more perishable market garden, fruit, and dairy products which they sold locally in Syracuse or shipped by rail to the larger urban markets of the East. A process of coalescence took place in county industries, with the firms in the city declining in number but growing larger in terms of the number of employees per firm and the average amount of capital invested in each firm.

Similar changes took place in hinterland firms, but the growth was more modest.

Economic changes such as these never take place in isolation; they occur, instead, within a social matrix made up of a constantly shifting population. The same transportation innovations that affected the economy of Onondaga County also influenced its people. It is to these people who lived in the city and its hinterland that we now turn our attention.

Notes

1. For a general discussion of the extension of the railroad system, see George Rogers Taylor, *The Transportation Revolution, 1815-1860* (New York: Holt, Rinehart and Winston, 1951).

2. Henry C. Van Schaack, *A History of Manlius Village* (Fayetteville, N.Y.: The Recorder Office, 1873), p. 13; H.C. Goodwin, *Pioneer History; or Cortland County and the Border Wars of New York* (New York: A.B. Burdick, 1859), p. 299.

3. William C. Redfield, *Sketch of the Geographical rout of a great railway,* second ed. (New York: G. & C. & H. Carvill, 1830), pp. 15-17; *American Railroad Journal,* July 14, 1832, May 12, 1832, and May 19, 1832; and Lewis H. Haney, *A Congressional History of Railways in the United States,* I (Madison: Democratic Printing Co., State Printer, 1908), pp. 224-226.

4. *Cayuga Patriot*, Auburn, New York, December 17, 1834.

5. See Fred Walker Stevens, *The Beginnings of the New York Central Railroad* (New York: G. P. Putnam's Sons, 1926); and *American Railroad Journal,* May 7, 1836, and June 11, 1836.

6. For further information on early railroads in Onondaga County, see Dwight H. Bruce, *Onondaga's Centennial: Gleanings of a Century,* I ([Boston]: The Boston History Company, 1896), pp. 227ff; Dwight H. Bruce, *Memorial History of Syracuse, from Its Settlement to the Present Time* (Syracuse: H.P. Smith & Co., 1891), p. 140; Richard F. Palmer, "The Skaneateles Railroad" (typescript, 1965, Syracuse Public Library); and *American Railroad Journal*, June 11, 1836.

7. See also Taylor, *The Transportation Revolution,* pp. 29-30; and *Daily Journal City Register and Directory for 1851-'52* (Syracuse: Daily Journal, 1851), pp. 55-58.

8. *American Railroad Journal*, July 3, 1845, November 6, 1845, and May 20, 1848; Stevens, *Beginnings of the New York Central*, p. 147; J. H.

French, *Gazetteer of the State of New York* (Syracuse: R. P. Smith, 1860), pp. 66-79.

9. Stevens, *Beginnings of the New York Central,* pp. 273ff; and Harlan W. Gilmore, *Transportation and the Growth of Cities* (Glencoe, Ill.: The Free Press, 1953), pp. 50-63.

10. Bruce, *Onondaga's Centennial*, I, pp. 886-88, and II, pp. 972-975.

11. Van Schaak, *History of Manlius Village,* pp. 10-11; E. Norman Leslie, *History of Skaneateles and Vicinity, 1781-1881* (Auburn: Charles P. Cornell, n.d. [before 1883]), p. 117; Bruce, *Onondaga's Centennial,* I, p. 655; Haney, *Congressional History of Railways,* I, pp. 238-239; Albert Fishlow, *American Railroads and the Transformation of the Ante-bellum Economy* (Cambridge: Harvard University Press, 1965), p. 18.

12. Quoted in Stevens, *Beginnings of the New York Central,* p. 149; see also *American Railroad Journal*, June 11, 1836, 353-354. Population data are taken from the United States Censuses of 1840, 1850, and 1860 and from Bruce, *Memorial History*, p. 611.

13. Asa Eastwood Papers, 1804-1872, George Arents Research Library, Syracuse University.

14. William B. Harris Journal (1837-1839), Department of Manuscripts and University Archives, Cornell University.

15. Data for calculating the estimated crude rate of natural increase are taken from the New York State Census, 1845 (see Chapter 3 for a description of the measure).

16. Thomas F. Gordon, *Gazetteer of the State of New York* (Philadelphia: printed for the author, 1836), pp. 577-586; and French, *Gazetteer,* pp. 472-490. The village of Skaneateles had lost its railroad five years earlier which undoubtedly affected the growth of the settlement's population.

17. For a general description of Onondaga agriculture, see Willis Gaylord, "Agriculture of Onondaga County" in *Transactions of the New York State Agricultural Society*, II (Albany: E. Mack, 1843), pp. 174-186; Russell H. Anderson, "New York Agriculture Meets the West, 1830-1850," *Wisconsin Magazine of History*, 16 (1932-1933), 163-198, 285-296; and George Geddes, *Report on the Agriculture and Industry of the County of Onondaga, State of New York* (Albany: Charles Van Benthuysen, 1860). All agricultural statistics are from the United States Census of Agriculture, 1850 and 1860, and the New York Census, 1845 and 1855, unless otherwise noted.

18. Geddes, *Report on Agriculture,* p. 116; and Bruce, *Onondaga's Centennial*, I, p. 883.

19. *Transactions of the New York State Agricultural Society*, 1849, p. 422, and 1853, pp. 525-526; Bruce, *Memorial History of Syracuse,* p. 675;

Bruce, *Onondaga's Centennial,* II, p. 962; and United States Census, 1850 and 1860.

20. *Transactions of the New York State Agricultural Society*, 1865, p. 469; and *Onondaga Standard*, June 15, 1852. Farmers also attempted to better their market situation by altering their methods of soil cultivation. There was a new interest in scientific farming after 1840, stimulated in part by the Onondaga County Agricultural Society which was formed that year. The agricultural society awarded annual prizes for superior farming and published detailed descriptions of winning farms in the organization's journal to give other farmers ideas on how to improve their own agricultural practices. Often science was used solely to measure seed, labor, and yields more carefully rather than to analyze improvements, although farmers also began to drain their land and to use manures as means of improving production. By 1846, conferences for farmers were being held in each township and an annual fair was held in Syracuse. See Gaylord, "Agriculture of Onondaga County," pp. 183-185, and *Transactions of the New York State Agricultural Society,* 1843, pp. 540-541, and 1846, p. 577.

21. Bruce, *Onondaga's Centennial,* I, p. 225; W. W. Clayton, *History of Onondaga County, New York* (Syracuse: Mason & Co., 1878), pp. 67-68; *American Railroad Journal*, February 27, 1845.

22. Johann Heinrich von Thünen, *The Isolated State*, translated by Carla M. Wartenberg and edited with an introduction by Peter Hall (Oxford and London: Pergamon Press, 1966).

23. List of Taxpayers in the Town of LaFayette, Onondaga County, 1827, Syracuse Public Library; Assessment Roll for the towns of Elbridge and Camillus, 1825, reprinted in Bruce, *Onondaga's Centennial*, I, pp. 673-677, 692-698; manuscript schedules of the United States Census of Agriculture, 1850, for Onondaga County; and New York State Census, 1855. The figures on farm size and value apply to farms producing crops valued at $100 or more. See Carroll D. Wright, *The History and Growth of the United States Census* (Washington: U.S. Government Printing Office, 1900).

24. The only exception to the decline in land values away from Syracuse is Elbridge, which had higher land values than Camillus in both 1850 and 1860, and Skaneateles in 1850.

25. Richard L. Ehrlich, "The Development of Manufacturing in Selected Counties in the Erie Canal Corridor, 1815-1860" (Ph.D. dissertation, State University of New York at Buffalo, 1972), pp. 213-214.

26. See Erhlich, "The Development of Manufacturing," p. 207, for a discussion of county industries.

27. Industrial statistics are taken from the New York State Census, 1855, unless otherwise noted.

28. The value of the products of industry, or value added to manufactured goods after processing, is calculated according to the formula $\frac{(A\text{-}B)}{B} \bullet 100$, where A is the value of the annual product and B is the value of the raw materials. The measure is a percentage of the original value of the raw materials. Data for these calculations were taken from the manuscript schedules of the federal Census of Industry, 1850 and 1860.

29. The wages of salt boilers were generally $30 per month in 1850, when the national average wage of industrial workers was only slightly over $20 per month. By 1860, however, salt workers' wages had dropped to $20 per month. During the same period, the average wage of industrial workers throughout the nation rose to $24. See the manuscript schedules of the federal Census of Industry, 1850 and 1860, and the U.S. Bureau of the Census, *Historical Statistics of the United States: Colonial Times to 1957* (Washington: U.S. Government Printing Office, 1960), p. 409.

30. Joshua V.H. Clark, *Onondaga; or Reminiscences of Earlier and Later Times,* II (Syracuse: Stoddard and Babcock, 1849), p. 218; and French, *Gazetteer*, pp. 472-490.

CHAPTER 5

The Social Component of Urban Growth: Migration to Syracuse

Initially part of the frontier, yet quickly becoming part of the settled portion of the United States as the frontier moved farther west, Onondaga County had a highly fluid population in the first half of the nineteenth century. Both in-migration and out-migration took place within various rural to urban, rural to village, intrarural and interurban migration streams. Although, as we have seen, the population of Syracuse continued to increase after 1830 and the rural areas experienced net out-migration, we have yet to examine the migration patterns that accomplished these changes. This chapter will focus on the population of Syracuse at mid-century, examining both local and long-range migration patterns that contributed to the growth of the city. The following chapter will discuss persistence and migration patterns in the county hinterland in order to identify migration alternatives as they were perceived by the nonurban majority in the nineteenth century.[1]

In 1820 a traveler, spending the night with Joshua Forman, a leading promoter of Syracuse, awoke to a dismal sight: "It was October," he later wrote, "and a flurry of snow during the night had rendered the morning aspect of the county more dreary than the evening before. The few houses, standing upon low and marshy ground, and surrounded by trees and tangled thickets, presented a very uninviting scene. 'Mr. Forman,' said I, 'do you call this a *village*? It would make an owl weep to fly over it'." This was Syracuse in the first months after the middle section of the Erie Canal was opened.[2]

Yet the traveler's pessimism was premature, for with the completion of the canal and the draining of the swamp between Syracuse and Onondaga Lake, the population of the "dreary" settlement jumped from 250 in 1820 to 2,565 people in 1830. As we have seen, the village at that time also boasted the county government buildings, a weighlock on the canal, and extensive warehouse facilities which could accommodate the growing quantities of goods and produce brought to Syracuse. It had, wrote visitor Robert J. Vandervater, "the appearance of New-York in miniature." By 1860, the city's dominance in the county was unmistakable; it contained 28,119 people or nearly one-third of the total population of Onondaga County.[3]

The rapid growth of the city's population after 1820 was not a result of the natural increase of the population, despite the fact that the crude rate of natural increase in the city was higher than in the surrounding hinterland. Rather, the expansion of the city was overwhelmingly due to in-migration. In 1855, only 2 percent of all heads of households in Syracuse had been born in the city, while the other 98 percent of the city's households were headed by first generation in-migrants.[4] (See Table 5.1.)

Table 5.1. **Birthplace of Syracuse Heads of Households, 1855**

	Number	Percent
Onondaga County		
Syracuse	94	2
Hinterland	315	7
New York State		
(excluding Onondaga)	961	20
Other U.S.	563	12
Outside U.S.	2,756	58
Unknown	43	1
Total	4,732	100

SOURCE: Manuscript Schedules, New York State Census, 1855.

One of the largest groups in the city was the foreign born. While about one-fourth of the state's population at the time was foreign born, fully 43 percent of the people of Syracuse were born outside of the United States—a higher proportion than found in Boston, a port city, at the same time. Moreover, the large component of foreign immigrant families in Syracuse is obscured by looking at the total population of the city.

Although native born residents—who comprised 57 percent of the city's population—were more numerous than the foreign born within the population as a whole in 1855, the profile of the city's residents by birthplace assumes a different shape among heads of household. Only four in ten of the city's households were headed by the native born, while roughly six in ten were headed by the foreign born. It is important to examine household heads in addition to the general population when looking at migration patterns, for each head of household represents the in-migration of an individual or a family. The large number of children born to foreign immigrants after their arrival in the United States were rightly counted as native born by the census enumerator, but these children were raised in immigrant households. (See Table 5.2 and Table 5.3.)

Irish immigrants had been living in the area since before Joshua Forman's disgruntled guest visited the settlement. Many originally came to Onondaga County as canal construction workers and remained to work in the salt springs after the canal was built. But in Syracuse as in other American cities, Irish immigration, particularly family immigration, increased tremendously in the 1840s and

Table 5.2. **Birthplace of Syracuse Residents, 1855**

	Entire Population, %	Household Heads, %
Foreign born	42	58
Native born	57	41

Source: Manuscript Schedules, New York State Census, 1855.

*Totals do not add up to 100 percent because some individuals did not know or would not give their place of birth when interviewed by the census taker.

Table 5.3. **Composition of the Population of Syracuse by Birthplace, 1855**

Birthplace	Number of Residents		Percent	
United States	14,416		57	
Onondaga County		8,313		33
New York (excluding Onondaga County)		4,261		17
New England		1,412		6
Other		430		2
Outside the United States	10,473		42	
Ireland		4,412		18
Germany		4,012		16
England		1,128		4
Canada		419		2
France		183		1
Scotland		89		0
Other		230		1
Unknown	218		1	
Total	25,107		100	

SOURCE: New York State Census, 1855.

the 1850s, and by 1855, the Irish made up 18 percent of the total population of the city. These later immigrants included people like Owen and Catharine O'Donald, who arrived in Syracuse in 1850 when they were 23 and 22 years of age. In 1855, Owen O'Donald worked as a laborer to support his wife and two American-born children, Mary and Margaretta. The O'Donalds shared their inexpensive frame house with another Irish family—Patrick and Mary Sherlock and their two children, who, like the O'Donald children, were born in Syracuse after their parents' arrival. In addition, the Sherlocks had a boarder living with them—8-year-old Bridgit Kelly, who was brought to Syracuse from Ireland at the age of one year. Many Irish families had a Canadian-born child as well as Irish- and American-born children because Irish immigrants frequently arrived in Canadian ports and made their way south to Syracuse by the Great Lakes and the Oswego Canal.[5]

The Germans, comprising 16 percent of the city's population in 1855, were nearly as numerous as the Irish. They too had been in the county since it had been first settled by Americans. Prior to the

1820s the majority of the German-born lived in the populous township of Manlius. By 1845, however, 85 percent of all German-born residents of Onondaga County lived in the township of Salina (which at that time still included the villages of Syracuse, Salina, Geddes, and Liverpool as well as a small portion of the surrounding agricultural areas). Ten years later, 71 percent of the German-born Onondagans lived in Syracuse itself. (See Table 5.4.) German immigrants to the city included skilled workers like Alexander Kasser, a shoemaker who came to Syracuse in 1848 at the age of 25. Two years later he married a German woman who had just arrived in the city. Their children, a girl, Barbara, and a boy, Alexander, were born in Syracuse. By 1855, Kasser had plied his trade in the city for seven years, was a naturalized citizen, and owned his own home. Despite the distance from his homeland, Kasser, like many American immigrants, lived near relatives, renting part of his home to an older brother and his family.[6]

The Irish and the Germans, like other foreign born migrants, came to Syracuse chiefly because of its favorable location astride the canals. Immigrants going west from ports in the northeastern United States tended to travel along the Erie Canal. Those arriving in Canada took the water route down the St. Lawrence River, along Lake Ontario, and down the Oswego Canal to its junction with the

Table 5.4. **Percentage of Each Major Foreign Nativity Group in Onondaga County Residing in the Township of Salina in 1845 and Syracuse in 1855**

	Salina 1845	Syracuse 1855
Canada		41
England	48*	30
Scotland		44
Ireland		47
France	58	44
Germany	85	71

SOURCE: New York State Census, 1845 and 1855.

*The figure for England in 1845 includes all of Great Britain.

Erie Canal. Both routes met in Syracuse, where many foreign born immigrants remained.

The transportation innovations of the period from 1820 to 1860, particularly the canals, encouraged the growth of the city's population by providing migrants with inexpensive transportation to Syracuse and by stimulating the city's economy so that it could, in turn, provide jobs for the growing urban population. This expansion of the city's population and its economy took place over the same period when large numbers of emigrants were leaving Ireland and Germany for the United States, providing many jobs for the new Americans. As it grew, Syracuse constantly required new workers in construction and wholesale and retail firms. Initially more important for the immigrants, however, was the continual need for unskilled laborers in the salt works. Because the work tending the fires under the salt vats was seasonal and very uncomfortable during the hot summer months, it was not attractive to the native born workers who could easily get better jobs in the city. By 1855, the salt boilers, the largest group of workers in Syracuse's most important industry, were almost entirely foreign born.

Just as many of the immigrants who flocked to Syracuse during these years arrived on canal boats from the north via the Oswego Canal and from the east on the Erie Canal, native born migrants to the city also came west across New York on the Erie Canal. The largest proportion of the native born in Syracuse, 33 percent of the city's total population, were born in Onondaga County. This group included most of the children in the city. In addition, 17 percent of the city's population had been born elsewhere in the state of New York—roughly the same proportion that had come to Syracuse from Ireland or from Germany. A much smaller proportion, 6 percent, had migrated to the city from the New England states with an additional 2 percent coming from other parts of the United States. (See Table 5.3.)

In 1855, the largest group of household heads, as opposed to all residents of the city, were those born in New York state but outside Onondaga County (20 percent of all heads of household). A further 12 percent of Syracuse heads of household were born elsewhere in the United States (largely in New England), and a mere 9 percent were born in Onondaga County. Three-fourths of the latter had been born in the county hinterland and later migrated to Syracuse. (See Table 5.1.)

In-state migrants (those born in New York State but not in Onondaga County) engaged in three distinct types of migration to Syracuse: short distance rural to urban migration; long distance rural to urban migration along major interregional transportation routes (primarily the Erie Canal); and city-hopping or migration from one city to another.[7]

The first migration pattern—short distance migration to Syracuse from the counties immediately surrounding Onondaga—was also the most common. Clearly, propinquity influenced migration patterns. Although the bulk of immigration from neighboring counties into Onondaga was to the Onondaga townships that bordered the county of origin, migration to Syracuse from each of these adjacent counties was next in importance. Despite the fact that Syracuse could not be considered a frontier city at this time, it profited from westward migration. More short distance moves to Syracuse were undertaken by people moving west from Madison County, directly to the east of Onondaga, than from any of the three counties to the north, south, or west of Onondaga. Even when the total number of emigrants from each county living in Syracuse in 1855 is computed as a proportion of the total home county population at earlier censuses (censuses that reflect the population of the counties at the time of out-migration), Madison County has the highest proportion of migrants to Syracuse. In short, the pull of the West influenced short distance migration flows far from the frontier.

The influence of direction on migration flows during this period can also be seen in the second pattern of migration to Syracuse—long distance rural to urban migration along major transportation routes. A large number of migrants came to Syracuse from homes in counties located along the route of the Erie Canal and the Hudson River. While the relatively cheap transportation the Erie Canal offered both stimulated migration and determined its path, such migration commonly took place only in a western direction. Counties to the west of Onondaga on the Erie Canal sent no more new residents to the city before 1855 than counties located far from the canals in other parts of the state.

A third pattern of migration to Syracuse was city-hopping or migration from one urban center to another—in this case, from New York City, Albany, Utica, Oswego, or Rochester to Syracuse. New York counties with large urban centers tended to send more Onondaga-bound migrants to Syracuse than counties without major cities. While there is no way to determine exactly that the migrants from these counties moved to Syracuse from other cities, the high proportion of migrants to Onondaga from counties with major cities who went to Syracuse, combined with the frequent mention of city-to-city migration in biographies of civic and business leaders in nineteenth-century Syracuse, suggests that city-hopping was a common form of migration. The impact of direction upon migration patterns was weaker in city-to-city migration than in rural-to-urban migration. The fact that there were more cities to the east of Syracuse than to the west meant that more urban-to-urban migrants came from eastern New York, but city-hopping also took place from cities to the west of Syracuse such as Rochester. For the city-hoppers, migration to Syracuse did not require learning how to cope in a new type of environment, but instead allowed them to use old skills advantageously in a new setting with new opportunities.

Although the migration patterns of Syracuse residents who came from states other than New York were more varied, most heads of household moving to Syracuse from New England arrived by way of the Erie and Oswego Canals. These New Englanders frequently traveled along the same paths as native born New Yorkers, many of them even living in eastern New York for several years before migrating to Onondaga County. Migrants from northern New England, however, crossed New York in a southwesterly direction, arriving in Syracuse from the north rather than going south to the Erie Canal and then west to Syracuse.

A final component of the city's population in 1855 was migrants to the city from the surrounding county hinterland (9 percent of all heads of household in 1855). Unlike the city-hoppers, these hinterland migrants had to learn a totally new set of economic skills in the city. Yet they were in a good position to adapt to new conditions since the journey to Syracuse was much shorter for them than for migrants who came from outside the county. In-county migrants were thus able to retain old social, family, and business ties while nurturing new relationships in the city. Migrants to Syracuse from other parts of Onondaga County were relatively young at the time of migration and had generally been engaged in high status occupations in their hinterland homes. Their decision to migrate to Syracuse was undoubtedly influenced by the fact that the city was the legal and commercial center of the county and offered more economic opportunities to its residents than other parts of the county.

To learn more about these migrants from the hinterland, we can use the manuscript schedules of the 1855 New York State Census for Syracuse to locate all heads of households who lived in the city but were born elsewhere in Onondaga County. In 1855, there were 303 heads of household born in the hinterland and living in the city. To examine migration to the city at different periods of time, these migrants can be divided into smaller groups according to decade of migration. (See Table 5.5.) The following analysis of hinterland migration to Syracuse will be based on separate examinations of Onondaga-born heads of household who arrived in Syracuse between 1851 and 1855, those who arrived between 1841 and 1850, and those who arrived between 1831 and 1840. Breaking down the analysis by time of migration will allow us to obtain maximum information from the most complete migrant population, those who arrived after 1850, as well as to note changes in the nature of hinterland migration to the city over time. A further advantage is that we can speculate on the long-range experiences of hinterland migrants in Syracuse by looking at the occupational characteristics

Table 5.5. **Time of Migration to Syracuse of Onondaga-born Syracusans, 1855 (Heads of Household in 1855)**

To 1819	6
1820-29	16
1830-39	57
1840-49	105
1850-59	139
Total	303

SOURCE: Manuscript Schedules, New York State Census, 1855.

of earlier migrant groups after five to twenty-five years of residence in the city.

A note of caution is in order here. Because the decadal migrant cohorts are composed only of in-migrants who remained in Syracuse from the time of migration until the 1855 census was taken, they are not necessarily representative of all hinterland migrants over the years. The most recent group of migrants, those arriving in Syracuse in the five-year period between 1850 and 1855, is the largest—not because immigration from the hinterland had necessarily increased but rather because so little time had elapsed to allow the new residents to migrate out of the city again. Descriptions of hinterland migration to Syracuse, then, are most representative when they describe these recent migrants. Analysis of earlier immigrant cohorts can suggest previous trends, but our conclusions must be carefully drawn since, because of attrition over time by death or outmigration, substantially smaller proportions of earlier migrant cohorts than later migrant cohorts were still resident in Syracuse in 1855. These caveats notwithstanding, the 303 migrants to Syracuse from the Onondaga hinterland shared similar experiences and illustrate many of the factors involved in migration from the hinterland to the city in the nineteenth century.

Geographical patterns of migration from the hinterland to Syracuse can be traced by locating the hinterland residences of migrants to the city. In the case of recent migrants this involved checking all Onondaga-born heads of households who by 1855 had lived in Syracuse five years or less against the manuscript schedules of the United States Census of 1850 for each township in the county. Migrants of five to thirty-five years' standing were similarly located using the 1840, 1830, and 1820 federal censuses. Of the individuals who moved to Syracuse between 1850 and 1855, over half, or 52 percent, could be located in 1850; 43 percent were then living in Onondaga County and 9 percent were living outside the county. (See Table 5.6.) Only 22 percent of the migrants of the 1840s and 26 percent of those who arrived in the 1830s could be traced to earlier homes in Onondaga County. The individuals who could not be located may simply have been missed by the census takers, who were very fallible, or they may have been living outside the county prior to moving into Syracuse.[8]

Table 5.6. **Migrants from the Onondaga County Hinterland to Syracuse, 1850-1855**

	Number	Percent
Located in 1850 county residence	60	43
Located in 1850 out-county residence	12	9
No information on residence prior to migration to Syracuse	67	48
Totals	139	100

SOURCE: Manuscript Schedules, United States Census, 1850.

The greatest number of hinterland migrants to Syracuse during the five-year period preceding 1855 came from the townships immediately surrounding the city. The negative correlation between a township's distance from Syracuse and out-migration to the city in the period between 1850 and 1855 is -.599, indicating that more than one-third of the migration to the city from the hinterland can be accounted for by the distance of the township of residence from Syracuse. However, since many of the townships located closest to the city were themselves populous and contained a larger pool of possible migrants than less densely settled towns, the same correlation should be calculated while controlling for population by township. This correlation is still -.563. The further Onondagans had to travel to get to Syracuse, the less likely they were to move there, even though the maximum distance from any township in the county to Syracuse was only twenty miles.

In addition to distance from Syracuse, another influence on hinterland migration was frequent economic contacts with the city. The townships of DeWitt and Onondaga, both adjacent to Syracuse, and the nearby township of LaFayette contributed more than one-third of the household heads who migrated to the city between 1850 and 1855. That these townships were leading suppliers of garden and dairy products to Syracuse residents emphasizes the importance of regular contacts with the city as a stimulus to urban migration. Perhaps equally important, however, was the presence of the Syracuse and Binghamton Railroad which was completed in 1854 and went north through these three townships before reaching Syracuse. (See Figure 7, p. 82.)

Regardless of where the hinterland migrants originally came from in the county, it was not unusual for Onondagans to migrate several times before moving to Syracuse. This serial or sequential migration could involve moves within the county or out of it before a move to Syracuse took place. Among Onondaga-born heads of household who moved into the city between 1850 and 1855, one in six came to Syracuse from another county. One-fourth of the Onondaga-born who migrated to Syracuse from outside the county came directly from Oswego County—usually from the city of Oswego.

A port on Lake Ontario and, like Syracuse, located midway between the Hudson River and Lake Erie, Oswego was also the northern terminus of the Oswego Canal. In 1855, its population was 15,816, and next to Syracuse it was the second largest city in the five county region (Onondaga and the four counties surrounding it). Because of easy transportation connections and frequent economic contacts between residents of the two cities, migration between the settlements was common. Typical of the Onondaga-Oswego migrants was N.H. McCrackin. Although born in Onondaga County, he established himself as a merchant in Oswego in the late 1830s and the 1840s. He returned to Onondaga County in 1854 when he moved to Syracuse at the age of 37. The city-hopping migration of McCrackin and other businessmen like him was indicative of the close economic ties among cities in central New York and also contributed to strengthening those ties.

Heads of households who moved with their families from the Onondaga hinterland to the city between 1850 and 1855 were generally young. In all, 76 percent of these adult migrants were between the ages of 20 and 39 at the time of migration, with the majority of this group between 30 and 39. None of the hinterland migrants in the five-year period was over the age of 60. However, by confining the study to heads of household, we have a group that is somewhat older than we would expect if we included all migrants to Syracuse from the hinterland. Household heads, as mentioned earlier, represent family migration decisions, and the fact that most heads of household were between the ages of 30 and 39 at the time of migration suggests that heads of families were moving to Syracuse after having worked for a number of years in the city's hinterland.

Migrants who arrived in Syracuse prior to 1850 appear at first glance to have been younger at the time of migration than the migrants between 1850 and 1855, with the majority of adult migrants to the city in the 1830s and 1840s having arrived between ages 20 and 29. However this difference in age is caused by the nature of the population being examined, which includes only individuals who were household heads in 1855. Since five to twenty-five years had elapsed between the time of migration and the census enumeration of 1855, the household heads who had migrated in the 1830s and 1840s undoubtedly included many who came as young, single migrants and married and became household heads after their arrival in Syracuse—making it appear that heads of households were migrating at an earlier age before 1850. In reality, age at migration probably was similar for both early and later migrants. We simply have a less exclusive group of migrants in terms of age and family status at migration from the earlier decades than we do from the 1850-1855 period.

In neither of these two earlier groups were there any migrants who had come to Syracuse after they reached the age of 50. This may simply be a reflection of the difficulties in trying to trace migrants five to twenty-five years after they migrated: the over-50 migrants to Syracuse may all have been dead by 1855. For similar reasons, it is almost impossible to learn about the age structure at the time of migration of pre-1830 hinterland immigrants to Syracuse from the few migrants of that period still remaining in the city in 1855. Most of these individuals came to the city as children, undoubtedly migrating within a larger family rather than as heads of households. Thirty-five years later (and in most cases even longer), none of their parents were still living in Syracuse, although it is not clear whether the parents of the youthful migrants emigrated from the city or whether they died before 1855.

More important than considerations of age and migration distance within the county is the socioeconomic status of hinterland migrants, for those who moved to Syracuse comprised an atypical cross section of the population. Farmers, who made up a majority of the adult male population in the hinterland, were underrepresented among migrants to Syracuse, for although agriculture was the principal economic activity in most hinterland townships, only 31 percent of those who migrated to Syracuse between 1850 and

1855 and could be traced to earlier hinterland residences were farmers prior to their migration. (See Table 5.7.) By 1855, when these same migrants were living and working in Syracuse, this proportion had declined because although the township of Syracuse included farmland on the fringes of the city, the migrating farmers from the hinterland clearly did not move to Syracuse to farm. Farmers who left hinterland townships for the city were most frequently drawn to business, white collar, and professional occupations and, secondly, to skilled labor. Only one farmer continued to farm on the outskirts of Syracuse after migrating from the hinterland. There was, however, a sizable group of former farmers living in Syracuse who registered no occupation at all with the census taker in 1855. These were not elderly farmers who may have sold their farms and retired to the city, but rather men who ranged in age from 23 to 50. They may have been temporarily out of work or perhaps they were engaged in urban land speculation, a particularly amorphous occupation in terms of census categories.

Like the farmers, unskilled workers filled a variety of new and more prestigious occupations in Syracuse. Although seven, or 15 percent, of the Onondaga heads of household who moved to the

Table 5.7. **Comparison of Occupations of Hinterland Migrants to Syracuse Before and After Migration**

Occupation	Hinterland, 1850		Syracuse, 1855	
	Number	*Percent*	*Number*	*Percent*
Unskilled labor	7	15	1	2
Skilled trades	4	8	9	19
Transportation industry	1	2	2	4
Salt industry			1	2
Business, white collar, and professional	21	44	25	52
Agriculture	15	31	3	6
Miscellaneous			1	2
None or unknown			6	13
Total	48	100	48	100

SOURCE: Manuscript Schedules, New York State Census, 1855, and United States Census, 1850.

city between 1850 and 1855 were unskilled workers in their hinterland homes, only one continued to work in an unskilled occupation in Syracuse. One of the former unskilled workers became a teacher, another an innkeeper, and still another a carpenter. Harry H. Henderson, who moved to Syracuse in 1851 at the age of 41, had been a cattle herder in the township of Onondaga, but once in the city, he became a deputy sheriff.

In addition to the occupationally mobile farmers and unskilled workers, there was an unusually high proportion of business, white collar, and professional people who migrated to Syracuse from the hinterland between 1850 and 1855. More than 43 percent of all hinterland migrants had been engaged in business, white collar, and professional occupations prior to migration. Among those who migrated to Syracuse when in their 30s, business, white collar, and professional people outnumbered all others. Significantly, the proportion of household heads whose occupations could be classified in this category increased after migration to 52 percent. Obviously, Syracuse offered great opportunities to hinterland residents with professional training or special skills, to those with the capital to open a new business, and to those with greater ambitions than their hinterland neighbors. It is equally clear that many residents of the county hinterland recognized the opportunities available and were able to take advantage of them.

Of the hinterland migrants to Syracuse in these white-collar occupations in 1855, more than half were engaged in business as merchants, manufacturers, hotel keepers, and millers. Their ties with the hinterland undoubtedly provided valuable customers for the difficult early years of new businesses. Manley L. Hilliard, for example, was a miller in Elbridge township until 1853, when he moved to Syracuse to operate a mill in the city. He presumably brought many of his Elbridge customers to his new place of business in the city. Similarly, a Manlius innkeeper, James Moulter, moved to the city in 1855 and became an urban hotel keeper.

In addition to those in business, many professionals migrated to Syracuse as did a smaller group of other white-collar workers. Men like Myron Wheaton, Charles O. Roundy, and Ansel E. Kinnee were teachers in Tully, Skaneateles, and DeWitt until they decided to move to Syracuse in the 1850s.

Hinterland lawyers exhibited the same village-to-city migration pattern illustrated by the teachers. Many young men from the hinterland received their legal training with a city lawyer; others, having read law in hinterland villages, migrated to the city soon after their training was completed. It was not unusual for lawyers to practice in a small village for several years before moving to the city, and many Onondaga villages repeatedly lost their lawyers to Syracuse. The fact that all county buildings were in Syracuse meant that most legal business was conducted there and that lawyers were in great demand in the city. Most migrant lawyers did not practice in the hinterland for long but moved to Syracuse while still in their 20s.[9]

Significant numbers of the hinterland residents who migrated to the city between 1830 and 1855 and who were heads of household in 1855 tended to occupy prestigious occupations in Syracuse. For example, 36 percent of those who migrated to Syracuse as adults in the 1840s and 23 percent of those who came to Syracuse as adults in the 1830s were employed in business, white collar, or professional jobs in 1855. (See Table 5.8.) Similarly, almost 35 percent of the hinterland migrants arriving between 1850 and 1855 were in business, white collar, or professional occupations in 1855. Of these recent migrants, those traceable to their earlier hinterland resi-

Table 5.8. **Occupations in 1855 of Adult Migrants to Syracuse from the Hinterland (in percent)**

Occupation, 1855	Decade of Migration		
	1830-1839	*1840-1849*	*1850-1855*
Unskilled labor	13	5	11
Skilled labor	23	23	25
Transportation	—	6	9
Salt industry	3	6	2
Business and the professions	23	36	35
Agriculture	6	4	4
Miscellaneous	3	8	2
None	29	13	12
Total	100	101	100
N	31	86	139

SOURCE: Manuscript Schedules, New York Census, 1855.

dences were more highly represented in business, white collar, or professional jobs (52 percent). The difference between the two groups, 17 percent, can be attributed to differences between those who could be traced to earlier hinterland residences at the time of migration to Syracuse and those who could not. This latter group, a total of 139 heads of household who were born in Onondaga County and moved to the city between 1850 and 1855, undoubtedly included many individuals who migrated several times before reaching the city in 1855 and were living outside the county in 1850. It is likely that this kind of serial migration out of Onondaga and eventually back to it stemmed from the individual's inability to achieve satisfactory economic or occupational rewards in any of his earlier residences; such a migrant might be expected to enter the urban labor force at a lower level than a hinterland resident who moved to the city with a satisfactory or successful work history. The addition of a group of migrants who may have been economically unsuccessful in earlier migrations could skew the occupational distribution of the entire group of recently migrated heads of households toward lower status occupations than exhibited by those who could be traced to previous hinterland residences.

Skilled urban workers far outnumbered unskilled workers among migrants to Syracuse from the Onondaga County hinterland. In the 1830s migrant cohort, 23 percent were skilled and 13 percent were unskilled in 1855, while in the 1840s group, the respective proportions were 23 and 5 percent. Of all hinterland migrants who arrived in Syracuse in the 1850s, 25 percent were engaged in skilled and only 11 percent in unskilled occupations in 1855. Some, like Alonso Vrooman, a mason in Geddes, followed the same vocations in the city as they had in their hinterland homes. Others left farming to take up skilled work in Syracuse. One of these was Cyrus Kinne, who became a carpenter in the city. Given the rapid physical expansion of the city in the 1850s, it is not surprising that the most numerous of the skilled workers among migrants from the hinterland between 1850 and 1855 were carpenters like Kinne; they were followed by tailors (male and female), coopers, and painters.[10]

Far fewer migrants from the hinterland worked in the salt works, which were, as mentioned earlier, dominated by foreign born immigrants to the city. Among migrants to Syracuse from the hinterland between 1850 and 1855, only 2 percent were employed as salt boilers, inspectors, and the like. Similarly low proportions of earlier migrants had found their way to employment in the salt works by 1855, with 6 percent of those who migrated to Syracuse from the hinterland in the 1840s and only 3 percent of those who arrived in the 1830s working at the salt works in 1855. Moreover, many of these men were in supervisory positions. (See Table 5.8.)

In general, the younger migrants from the hinterland to the city were found in 1855 in occupations calling for less training and capital than the occupations of those who were somewhat older at the time of migration. Controlling for age among hinterland migrants to Syracuse in the 1850s, we see that the largest occupational category of young migrants between the ages of 20 and 29 at the time of migration was skilled worker (35 percent), with business, white collar, and professional occupations next among young household heads (28 percent). The situation is sharply reversed among those who migrated between the ages of 30 and 39 and between 40 and 49. Nearly two-thirds of all those in their 30s when they migrated were in business, white collar, and professional or in skilled occupations in 1855, with 44 percent in the first category and 20 percent in the second. The same pattern is evident among recent migrants in their 40s. (See Table 5.9.) Hinterland migrants who were over 50 at the time of migration exhibited a scattering of occupations, without any clear pattern. It is likely that those who migrated after the age of 50 did so for a variety of personal reasons rather than in response to the economic opportunities that attracted so large a number of younger people.

Among migrants who arrived in Syracuse prior to 1850, age was less important in distinguishing between individuals in business, white collar, or professional, and skilled occupations in 1855. Of those who migrated to Syracuse from the hinterland in the 1840s, business, white collar, and professional occupations were more numerous by 1855 in both younger age groups (20-29 and 30-39) than other types of occupations. However since by 1855 five to fifteen years had elapsed since the time of migration, the preponderance of businessmen and professionals could suggest that these individuals found Syracuse more profitable than did other migrants from the hinterland and were perhaps less likely than

Table 5.9. **Occupation in 1855 by Date of Migration and Age at Migration to Syracuse**

Occupation	1840-1849		1850-1855		
	20-29	*30-39*	*20-29*	*30-39*	*40-49*
Unskilled labor	6	—	15	12	5
Skilled labor	28	15	35	20	14
Transportation	4	10	13*	5	9
Salt industry	7	—	—	3	5
Business and the professions	39	50	28	44	32
Agriculture	2	—	2	3	5
Miscellaneous	—	10	2	—	9
None	6	10	4	12	23
Unknown	9	5	—	—	—
Total	101	100	99	99	102
N	54	20	46	59	22

Source: Manuscript Schedules, New York Census, 1855.

*All employed by the railroads.

other immigrants of that decade to leave the city at a later date. It is probable too that the younger migrants were adaptable and able to respond to the economic opportunities of the city, given five to fifteen years to do so. Over time, this receptivity coupled with increased city contacts may have given those who migrated while young a competitive advantage by 1855 that many older migrants lacked. If so, the young migrants who arrived in the early 1850s could be expected to move in time to more demanding and rewarding occupations as well.

Whether the general occupational mobility demonstrated by the hinterland migrants to Syracuse between 1830 and 1855 was a typical phenomenon during the first half of the nineteenth century awaits the results of further research. It is likely, however, that the occupational success of urban migrants was dependent upon the structure of the city's economy and the migration alternatives perceived by potential migrants. In his study of rural migration to Reading, Pennsylvania, John Modell found that hinterland migrants were most apt to turn to unskilled labor after moving to the city—a sharp contrast to the experiences of Onondaga migrants to Syracuse. However Reading was an industrial city, while Syracuse was primarily a commercial and transportation center. Because they had different economic bases, the structure of the labor market in the two cities was also different. New job opportunities in Reading were the result of industrial expansion that provided jobs for factory workers, while in Syracuse the commercial and physical expansion of the city most often led to new opportunities in white collar and skilled construction work. In Syracuse, moreover, the foreign born dominated the lower ranks of the salt industry, which consumed the largest numbers of unskilled laborers in the city and might otherwise have attracted unskilled workers from the county hinterland. A final reason for the absence of large numbers of unskilled laborers among hinterland migrants to Syracuse is the ease with which unskilled Onondagans could migrate to better farmlands in the West via the Erie Canal if the economic opportunities in the city did not appeal to them. In contrast, farmland to the west of Reading deteriorated in quality for nearly 200 miles, and western migration was considerably more difficult.[11]

In sum, transportation innovations contributed to the growth of the city of Syracuse by stimulating its economy, as we have seen in Chapters 3 and 4, and by attracting and carrying migrants to the city as this chapter has shown. By 1855, Syracuse was a city of young urban immigrants and their families. In addition to the immigration of the foreign born, there was much short distance migration to Syracuse from the immediately adjacent counties (particularly from those counties to the east of Onondaga) and a sizable population movement to the city from New England and counties in eastern New York along the Erie Canal and the Hudson River. A third form of migration from within the state was city-hopping, or migration to the growing city of Syracuse from other cities, mainly New York, Albany, Utica, Oswego, and Rochester.

There was also a small but significant stream of migration from the Onondaga County hinterland to the city of Syracuse. These migrants were characteristically engaged in high status and highly rewarded occupations both in the township of migration and, to an even greater extent, in the city after migration. Even those who were engaged in farming or unskilled occupations before moving to Syracuse generally occupied business, white collar, and professional or skilled occupations after their move to the city. In short, migration to Syracuse from the hinterland frequently involved occupational as well as geographical mobility.

While Syracuse undoubtedly benefited from the immigration of hinterland residents, their out-migration from hinterland townships constituted a drain of talent, skill, and capital to the city. Since it was the people in the upper levels of the socioeconomic hierarchy in rural and village Onondaga who moved to Syracuse, their loss, together with the loss of capital they represented, inevitably weakened the economy of the hinterland and made it more dependent upon Syracuse.

Even hinterland residents who did not migrate to Syracuse often invested in urban real estate as the city grew; in this way, they contributed hinterland capital to the growth of the city just as migrating businessmen brought investment capital to Syracuse. Investment in urban land was most common in townships close to the city such as Manlius and, after 1835, DeWitt, a township formed when Manlius was divided in two. For example, 5 percent of a systematic random sample of household heads in the township of Manlius in 1830 invested in Syracuse land between 1820 and 1860. Smaller proportions of similar samples taken in Lysander and Fabius invested in urban land over the same period (1 percent and 3 percent, respectively). The lower rate of investment from these two townships was probably due to the greater distance between them and Syracuse. Although one former Manlius resident in the sample who had moved to Syracuse returned to the hinterland to purchase land in DeWitt township, this reverse pattern was rare. When affluent Syracusans began to think in terms of purchasing out-of-town property for investment or recreation, they turned north to Brewerton, a village on Lake Oneida, rather than to the townships of the agricultural hinterland.[12]

The migration to the city of those with special skills was only a fraction of the total population movement taking place in the hinterland. In addition to the migrants leaving for Syracuse, there was another, considerably larger, stream of migrants moving out of the county hinterland between 1820 and 1860. These people saw a better future in less familiar cities and in other rural areas which they felt offered more opportunities than Onondaga County. In fact, the very transportation innovations, particularly the Erie

Canal, that brought migrants from the east to Syracuse also facilitated out-migration from the Onondaga County hinterland of Syracuse. They provided cheap transportation to newly developing areas in the West—areas that were economically viable because the same transportation innovations enabled western farmers to market their grains in the urban centers of the East.

Notes

1. For a detailed discussion of the literature on migration theory, see Allan Pred, *The External Relations of Cities During "Industrial Revolution"; with a Case Study of Göteborg, Sweden, 1868-1890* (Chicago: University of Chicago, Department of Geography Research Paper #76, 1962), pp. 57-68; Everett S. Lee, "A Theory of Migration," *Demography* 3 (1966), 47-57; and E.G. Ravenstein, "The Laws of Migration," *Journal of the Royal Statistical Society*, 48 (1885), 167-227, and 52 (1889), 241-301.

2. This anecdote was printed in the Syracuse *Journal,* December 12, 1872; Franklin Chase, *Syracuse and Its Environs,* I (New York: Lewis Historical Publishing Company, 1924), p. 411.

3. Robert J. Vandervater, *The Tourist, or Pocket Manual for Travellers*. . . 3rd ed. (New York: Harper & Brothers, 1834), p. 56.

4. Population statistics, unless otherwise noted, are taken from the New York State Census of 1855.

5. One of the leading merchants in Salina and later in Syracuse was Thomas McCarthy, an Irish immigrant who opened a store near the salt springs as early as 1808. See the manuscripts of the New York State Census of 1855 for Syracuse for evidence of Canadian-born infants of Irish parentage. See also, Maldwyn A. Jones, *American Immigration* (Chicago: University of Chicago Press, 1960).

6. See Dwight H. Bruce, *Memorial History of the City of Syracuse* (Boston: H. P. Smith & Company, 1891), pp. 336-363. German settlement was heavily concentrated in certain sections of the city, such as the second ward, which contained almost no non-German families. See also the manuscript schedules of the New York State Census of 1855 for Syracuse.

7. Migration as used here involves the trip from place of birth to place of residence in 1855.

8. Individuals were located through indices to the federal censuses of 1800 to 1850 which can be found in the Syracuse Public Library and the Onondaga Historical Association. Since censuses prior to 1850 enumerated only the head of household by name, individuals who were not of this

status at the time of the census could not be located. The census materials were supplemented by genealogical research aids in both repositories. Some of the missing 48 percent of the migrants to Syracuse from 1850 to 1855 were probably still in Onondaga County and were simply missed by the census taker. Others were undoubtedly living outside the county immediately prior to migration. Repeated migrations were common, and even among the migrants who could be traced, one in six lived outside the county before moving to Syracuse. These people were generally located through genealogical materials rather than the census records. If the census for each New York county could be searched, many of the remaining migrants would doubtless be located; a systematic search of the census manuscript records for the other 59 counties was, of course, impossible.

9. Mary Ellis Maxwell, *Among the Hills of Camillus* (n.p., 1952); see also manuscript schedules for Syracuse of the 1855 New York State Census.

10. Female heads of household made up 10.1 percent of the 1850-1855 migrant group. Although six, or nearly half the group, gave no occupation, an equal number were tailoresses or seamstresses and were classified as skilled workers for this analysis. None of the female heads of households were in the largest occupational group of business, white collar, and professional occupations. Most women migrated to the city as the spouse of the head of household.

11. John Modell, "The Peopling of a Working-Class Ward: Reading, Pennsylvania, 1850," *Journal of Social History*, 5 (1971), 71-95.

12. For more information on the samples of Manlius, Lysander, and Fabius, see Chapter 6. The total number of hinterland investors in urban real estate in the three samples was ten; six of these were from Manlius. See Joshua V. H. Clark, *Onondaga; or Reminiscences of Earlier and Later Times,* II (Syracuse: Stoddard and Babcock, 1848), pp. 174-179, for further information on urban investment in Brewerton and the growth of the village as a watering place for urban residents.

CHAPTER 6

The Response of the Hinterland: Persistence and Migration

The first few years after the construction of the Erie Canal were, as we have seen, a time of rising expectations for residents of rural Onondaga. For the people who had worked so long and hard to establish the farms, stores, and mills that dotted the countryside, recovery from the Panic of 1819 and the stimulation of the new marketing patterns created by the canal together led to a climate of great optimism throughout the county in the early 1820s. True, business in the turnpike villages was slack, but this initially was seen as a temporary phenomenon to be endured until the necessary feeder canals were built to connect these settlements with the canal system and prosperity. However reality has a strange way of failing to meet expectations. Instead of expansion, the decades following 1820 saw a gradual lowering of the ceiling on economic opportunities in the rest of Onondaga County. Agriculture came to dominate most of the county to the exclusion of other economic activities, although a few villages remained important and even began to grow by 1830 as hinterland oases with more diverse economies than the surrounding areas. Throughout the period from 1820 to 1860, there was a drain of capital and entrepreneurial talent to Syracuse from the hinterland. The crude rate of natural increase declined, and out-migration began to exceed in-migration.

The study of persistence and out-migration provides another valuable index to the degree to which economic changes in the county affected the population of the city's hinterland. During this period, the location of Onondaga County, its access to the canal and fertile western land, permitted residents to translate economic dissatisfactions into action through migration to another, hopefully better, place. In addition, the study of persistence and migration can also reveal where social ties filtered and modified the direct response to economic change—at times stimulating and at times retarding the emigration of individuals. In short, out-migration from the hinterland was the result of a complex of social and economic factors, the dimensions of which will be explored in this chapter.

The study of out-migration from the hinterland should be approached in three ways. First, it is necessary to explain why out-migration exceeded in-migration during and after the 1830s. Second, it is useful to look at the rate and pattern of out-migration from Onondaga County over time to determine whether migrants came from all parts of the hinterland community and whether their leaving changed the composition of the hinterland appreciably. Finally, an examination of the nature of the social and economic background of the out-migrants might help us to understand why so many individuals left the hinterland.

Overall, as we have seen, patterns of population growth and decline in Onondaga County townships changed rapidly and dramatically between 1820 and 1860. The decades of the 1820s and the 1840s were years of population growth for the county as a whole, while the 1830s and the 1850s were periods of considerably less growth. Not coincidentally, both the 1830s and the 1850s witnessed great surges in land sales in the western states. The city of Syracuse outstripped its hinterland in total population growth and in-migration during the entire period, and, after 1830, in natural increase as well. As early as the 1820s, out-migration from the townships of the county hinterland exceeded in-migration, although a high rate of natural increase assured these townships of limited population growth until the 1830s. While certain sections of the most sparsely settled northern part of the county continued to grow in the 1840s, the number of hinterland townships with an absolute population loss had risen from three to seven, and in the 1850s, the hinterland as a whole recorded an absolute population loss.[1]

Yet only a limited amount of information on persistence and migration patterns can be obtained from the aggregate population statistics published in the decennial federal census reports and the state census reports which were taken at the mid-decade point. In order to go beyond a superficial analysis of population change, the residential movements of individual Onondagans must be examined over a long period of time. To do this, I have taken three systematic samples of household heads from the manuscript schedules of the 1830 federal census of households in the hinterland townships of Manlius, Fabius, and Lysander. (See Figure 5, p. 48.) Although the three townships were different in terms of location, original population, and access to interregional transportation systems, each was typical of a number of other Onondaga townships. Taken together, their experiences illustrate the effects of transportation innovations, economic change, and urban growth upon the Onondaga hinterland populations.[2]

Of the three townships, Manlius was settled first. It was, in fact, one of the earliest townships in the county to be inhabited by whites, and it boasted several vigorous settlements by the first decade of the nineteenth century. Later, both the Erie Canal and the Syracuse and Utica Railroad passed through the center of the township, giving Manlius transportation advantages many other townships lacked. In addition, Manlius was located directly to the east of Syracuse, and the township's residents had close economic ties with the city. In 1835, the original township of Manlius was divided into two townships, Manlius and DeWitt. For the purposes of this analysis, however, the two will continue to be considered as a single unit, since a person living in Manlius in 1834 could be living in DeWitt in 1836 without ever having changed his residence.

Unlike Manlius, Fabius was located away from interregional transportation routes. Situated in the southeastern corner of the county, Fabius was a farming area with hills and hollows that originally attracted the overflow of Yankee settlers from the townships of Pompey and Manlius to the north. Between 1830 and 1840, the population of Fabius declined; thereafter, it experienced a relatively slight but stable decline each decade. Its settlements did not expand beyond their pre-1820 size, and the township remained predominantly agricultural throughout the antebellum period.

Lysander, the third township to be sampled, was located in the northern part of Onondaga County and was settled later than Manlius and Fabius. Despite the fact that the thriving village of Baldwinsville was in this township, Lysander was one of the most sparsely settled areas of Onondaga in the 1830s. Because it had a large supply of uncultivated land long after most other townships with superior and better-drained soils had been fully settled, Lysander continued to attract migrants from both within and outside the county until the 1850s.

Although the settlement of Onondaga County had begun forty years earlier, many residents were still newcomers in 1830. Nearly one-third, 32 percent, of the combined samples of household heads in 1830 had lived in the same township in 1820, while an additional 7 percent of the sample members had lived elsewhere in Onondaga ten years earlier. Excluding those between the ages of 20 and 29 in 1830 (and likely to have been living in their parents' households in 1820 rather than in their own households), we find that 41 percent of the remaining sample members had lived in the township of enumeration in 1820 and 9 percent in other Onondaga townships. A total, then, of 50 percent of all sample members 30 years of age and over in 1830 had been in Onondaga County for the ten years which saw the construction of the Erie Canal and the initial growth of the canal village of Syracuse. The other half of the sample population arrived in Onondaga sometime after the middle section of the Erie Canal had been completed.[3]

By the end of the following decade, however, out-migration had reduced the sample population considerably. In 1840, only four out of every ten sample members still resided in the township of enumeration. The remainder of the sample had either left the township or died between 1830 and 1840. Using appropriate model life tables to approximate mortality during the decade, we can further estimate that overall mortality for sample members under the age of 70 was 16 percent. Excluding those who are likely to have died between 1830 and 1840, we have an estimated 43 percent of the sample migrating before 1840. (See Table 6.1.) The extent of migra-

Table 6.1. **Persistence, Migration, and Age, 1830-1840 (in percent)**

Age	Persisters	Expected to Die in Decade	Estimated Migrants
20-29	32	7	62
30-39	44	9	47
40-49	44	15	41
50-59	36	27	37
60-69	42	47	10

SOURCE: Sample data.

tion among household heads in the samples suggests that despite the economic advantages that improved interregional transportation brought to Onondaga County in the 1830s, many residents of the hinterland felt they had a better future in other places—within the county or outside it.[4]

In the 1840s, however, migration by sample members declined substantially. Of all sample members still present in the township of enumeration in 1840, 57 percent were also present in 1850. This was 23 percent of the original sample. Given an overall estimated mortality in this decade of 22 percent for all those under the age of 70, only 17 percent of the persisters of the 1830s probably emigrated from the township of enumeration between 1840 and 1850, as compared to 43 percent in the decade of the 1830s. (See Table 6.2.) The sharp drop in the migration rate from the first to the second decade after the sample was taken was undoubtedly due to the greater tendency of people to move after short periods of

Table 6.2. **Persistence, Migration, and Age, 1840-1850 (in percent)**

Age	Persisters	Expected to Die in Decade	Estimated Migrants
30-39	73	9	18
40-49	59	15	26
50-59	68	27	6
60-69	41	47	11

SOURCE: Sample data.

residence than after lengthier periods. By the 1840s, all remaining sample members had been living in the same township for at least ten years and were less likely to move than they had been earlier.

Hinterland residents engaged in three major forms of migration between 1820 and 1860: local, short range migration to nonurban locations, including other townships in Onondaga County; migration to urban centers; and western migration.

A common form of migration in the 1830s was short range migration to other Onondaga hinterland townships. Of all sample members who left the township of enumeration during the decade, 7 percent (or approximately 4 percent of the entire sample) moved to other locations in the county hinterland. (See Table 6.3.) The most frequent move was to an adjacent township, with 5 percent of the migrating sample members moving to contiguous hinterland townships. This pattern of short range migration to nearby and familiar places was even more evident in the migrations of members of the First Presbyterian Church of Marcellus during the 1830s. Almost a third, 32 percent, of all church members who transferred their church membership in the 1830s left Marcellus for other Onondaga locations, and of these, 63 percent moved to adjacent townships—a considerably higher proportion than among sample members who moved to other county locations. The smaller

Table 6.3. **Migration in the 1830s (in percent)**

	Manlius	Fabius	Lysander	Combined samples
Migrants to Syracuse	10	2	2	5
Migrants to other parts of county hinterland	6	8	6	7
Migrants outside Onondaga County	10	9	—	7
Known to have died in 1830s	8	3	5	5
Disappeared without trace	66	78	88	77
Total	100	100	101	101
N	67	65	65	197

SOURCE: Sample data.

proportions of in-county migrants and migrants to adjacent townships among sample members than among church members suggests that short distance moves were more frequently undertaken by people with institutional affiliations in the community—such as church membership—than by the general population, as represented by the 1830 sample members.[5] (See Table 6.4.)

Table 6.4. **Migrants from First Presbyterian Church, Marcellus, in the 1830s (in percent)**

Destination	All Migrants	Males	Females
Elsewhere in Onondaga County	32	28	34
Elsewhere in New York State	17	20	14
Out of the state	48	48	49
Unknown	3	4	3
Total	100	100	100
N	60	25	35

SOURCE: "Church Records from First Presbyterian, St. John's Episcopal and Methodist Churches," Syracuse Public Library.

A second tendency in short range, local migration was the movement of county migrants away from the east-west transportation routes to townships in the northern and southern parts of the county. This tendency was probably related to the rising cost of land. Farmers who were experiencing financial difficulties and prospective farmers who wanted to remain in the region could find cheaper land in townships further away from the Erie Canal. In the 1820s, county migrants moved to both the northern and southern parts of the county. Examination of the in-migration patterns to Lysander, Fabius, and Manlius in that decade suggests not only that local migrants were avoiding Manlius and other of the early and most well-settled townships in the center of the county (most of which were also on the interregional transportation routes—canal or turnpike), but that people were, in addition, leaving these townships for new homes in both Fabius and Lysander, townships which were farther from the turnpikes and the Erie Canal. By the

1830s, migration away from the heavily settled transportation routes was directed largely to the northern tier of the county townships—particularly to Lysander, which was attractive to migrating Onondagans because it had relatively cheap land and a growing village, Baldwinsville, to attract new settlers. In this decade, townships like Fabius in the southern part of the county were beginning to lose population, possibly because of the expansion of dairying in the southern townships that supported fewer farmers on a given number of acres.

The second form of hinterland migration in the 1830s, migration to Syracuse or urban migration, was less common than migration to other hinterland townships. These urban migrants, described in detail in the previous chapter, were the sole exception to the general tendency of in-county migrants to avoid the canal and turnpike townships in this decade. However migrants to Syracuse from the three hinterland townships in the sample comprised only 5 percent of the non-persisters of the 1830s. Not surprisingly, most of these came from Manlius rather than from Fabius or Lysander. As we saw in Chapter 5, migrants tended to move westward along interregional transportation routes more frequently than in other directions, and Syracuse was located on the Erie Canal to the west of Manlius. In addition, the short distance between Syracuse and Manlius (and, after 1835, between Syracuse and DeWitt), undoubtedly encouraged this movement.

Migration within Onondaga County was only a part of the population movement taking place in and out of the county hinterland, for a much larger group of sample members was moving out of the county. Unfortunately, tracing the individuals who actually left the county during this decade is far more difficult—and far less profitable—than following those who migrated to other locations within Onondaga County. Since information about emigration and subsequent residence comes primarily from genealogical records, there is an element of chance involved in tracing out-migration, with a clear bias toward emigrants who settled permanently or for long periods of time in one place. For example, the fact that no out-county migration was traceable from Lysander indicates the sparseness of the data rather than the absence of emigration. It is very likely that the 7 percent of non-persisting sample members who could be traced to new residences in other parts of New York and outside the state were only a fraction of the migrants who left Onondaga County entirely. When we turn to a population we can trace—the sixty migrants from the First Presbyterian Church of Marcellus in the 1830s—we find that 65 percent moved out of Onondaga County. Although many of these migrated to adjacent counties and westward along the Erie Canal to other canal cities, approximately three-quarters of the church members who left the county moved to the western states. (See Table 6.4.) The destinations of these Presbyterians suggests that most of the 77 percent of the sample members who disappeared during the 1830s without leaving traces for future historians or genealogists to follow also moved west. The available data on sample members from Manlius and Fabius confirm this pattern.[6]

Because the Erie Canal provided easy transportation to the Great Lakes States, the most frequent destination of Onondaga migrants during the 1830s was Michigan, followed by Illinois and Ohio. These western states offered Onondagans fertile land at low prices at a time when Onondaga land was both becoming exhausted and, because of improvements to the land and buildings and the gradual inflation of land values in settled areas, rising in price. Israel Parsons, the historian of early Marcellus, wrote that so many local residents departed for Michigan—only a week's journey from Onondaga County—that whole sections of the township were left deserted. The enthusiasm and excitement of would-be migrants was called the "Michigan Fever," and it infected whole neighborhoods with the urge to migrate. One settlement in Ingham County, Michigan, became the new home of so many transplanted Onondagans that a former Fabius resident, Orange Phelps, named the village Onondaga.

In the following decade (1840 to 1850), changes in the migration patterns of sample members suggest that there were differences between the migration patterns of recent and long-term residents. Short distance moves within the county hinterland were most frequent among recent migrants while long-term residents, when they migrated, tended to move greater distances. Members of the samples of the hinterland population in 1830 did not move within the county as much between 1840 and 1850 as they had in the 1830s.

Although 11 percent of the non-persisters of the 1830s moved to other county locations (including Syracuse), only 6 percent of the non-persisters of the 1840s did so. Moreover, all of the sample members who remained in the township of enumeration for at least twenty years before migrating moved out of the county, usually to the western states.

The same phenomenon can be seen in the migrations of Marcellus church members in the 1830s: recently arrived residents, identified through the brevity of their church membership, tended to move short distances within the county, while long-term residents tended to move outside the county and outside the state. Half the migrants who had been church members five years or less (and presumably Marcellus residents for the same period of time) moved to other Onondaga County locations in the 1830s, while none of the migrants who had previously lived in Marcellus longer than fifteen years moved within the county. This inverse relationship between short-range migration and length of residence suggests that in-county moves were most frequently made close to the time of initial settlement in the county, if they were made at all, and that these moves should be considered part of the initial process of settlement for migrants to the county. (See Table 6.5.)

The factors which led to the persistence or migration of hinterland residents were generally independent of the rapid growth of Syracuse in the antebellum period. The appeal of the city to potential migrants, discussed in Chapter 5, did not motivate large numbers of Onondagans in the hinterland to move to Syracuse. A commitment to farming and a familiarity with rural and village living inhibited most heads of household in the hinterland from moving to the busy city. In contrast, the cheap, fertile lands in the West seemed very desirable, particularly when, as we have seen, Onondaga land was becoming both less fertile and continually more expensive. Ultimately, individuals decided to migrate because of a mixture of personal factors such as the desire for more or better land than was available in Onondaga County, kinship and family ties either in Onondaga or in the West, and stage of life.

Landholding patterns affected both persistence and migration in the county hinterland more than any other factor. Although both landowners and non-landowners emigrated from the three hinter-

Table 6.5. **Length of Residence in Onondaga County and Destination at Time of Migration, 1830s**

Length of Residence at Time of Migration	*N*	Destination			
		Within Onondaga County	*Elsewhere In New York*	*Out of the State*	*Unknown*
5 years or less	26	13	5	7	1
6-10 years	8	4	1	3	—
11-15 years	11	2	1	7	1
16-20 years	10	—	3	7	—
21 years and over	5	—	—	5	—

Source: "Church Records from First Presbyterian, St. John's Episcopal and Methodist Churches," Syracuse Public Library.

land townships during the 1830s, there was a much higher proportion of landless household heads among sample members who emigrated (44 percent) than among those who remained in the same township throughout the decade (17 percent). Or, to turn the figures around, only 56 percent of the sample members who migrated were landowners, while fully 83 percent of the persisters owned land. Although the proportion of the landless was higher among migrants than among persisters in all three townships, there were proportionately more migrant landowners in Fabius than in the other two townships and fewer migrating landowners in Lysander. This was due to the overall differences in the proportion of landowners among sample members in the three townships, for the proportion of landholders among migrants was obviously related to the overall proportion of landholders in the township. In Fabius, for example, at least 77 percent of all sample members owned land at some time and 66 percent of all migrants were landowners. (See Table 6.6.) In contrast to Fabius, only 54 percent of the Lysander sample and a mere 42 percent of the Lysander migrants ever owned land. Manlius's figures are between the other two townships. The ratio of the proportion of landowners among migrants to the

Table 6.6. **Landownership among Migrants, 1830-1839 (in percent)**

	Manlius	Fabius	Lysander
No evidence of landownership	40	34	58
Evidence of landownership	57	66	42
Uncertain evidence of landownership	3		
Total	100	100	100
N	62	62	63
Ratio of proportion of landowners among migrants to proportion of landowners among total sample	85.0	86.1	77.0

SOURCE: Sample data.

proportion of landowners in the entire sample is somewhat lower in Lysander than in Fabius and Manlius, however, suggesting that landowners in Lysander were slightly less likely to migrate than landowners in the other townships. This may reflect the fact that Lysander landowners were able to expand their holdings after 1830 to a greater extent than their counterparts in Manlius and Fabius because of the greater supply of undeveloped land in Lysander.[8]

Not only were persisters more likely to own land than non-persisters, but persisting landowners were probably more prosperous than most Onondaga landowners in the 1830s and thus had a greater economic incentive to remain in Onondaga County. Although there are no comparative data for the townships of Manlius and Fabius, the Lysander Tax Assessment Roll for 1835 supports this contention. While the mean size of landholdings among landowning sample members in Lysander in 1830 was 71.3 acres in 1835, those landowners who migrated during the decade owned an average of only 57.4 acres. Moreover, landowning sample members who remained in Lysander through the decade held an average of 78.0 acres each in 1835—an average of 20.6 acres more per landowning persister than per landowning migrant.

Fifteen years later, in 1850, landowning persisters in Manlius and Fabius held, on the average, slightly more land than the mean landhold for each township, although this was not true in Lysander. Landowning persisters in Lysander had increased the average size of their farms from 78.0 to 93.5 acres by 1850. However the mean size of all Lysander farms had increased much more than the farms of sample members, jumping from 56.6 acres to 93.3 acres and essentially closing the gap between persisting farm owners in the sample taken in 1830 and all farm owners in the township regardless of length of tenure. This was not the case in Manlius and Fabius, where long residence in the township by sample members meant larger than average farms in 1850. At that time, sample members still owned an average of 89 acres in Manlius, while the average farm in the township was only 84 acres. Similarly in Fabius, twenty-year persisters owned farms averaging 124 acres while the township mean was only 117 acres. The discrepancy between Lysander and the other two townships is probably due to the later settlement and extension of farmland in Lysander which made it possible to purchase large parcels of land at a time when this was difficult to do in the other two townships. Between 1835 and 1850, the total number of acres of improved land increased by 70 percent in Lysander but only by 23 percent in Manlius and 17 percent in Fabius.[9]

Kinship or family ties also affected both persistence and migration in the Onondaga County hinterland. As indicated in Chapter 2, kinship relationships were important factors in determining where individuals settled during the initial peopling of the county before 1820, and they continued to exert an influence on settlers in later years. Kinship ties affected Onondaga residents in two ways. First, the migration of a single person or family in a kinship network acted as a stimulus upon the remaining Onondaga relatives to emigrate and join their kin. At the same time, however, kinship ties could also have the opposite effect and often retarded the emigration of families with close kinship ties in their Onondaga township. The reinforcement of persistence by kinship relationships in Onondaga County may not be unusual. In studying the effect of kinship relationships upon residents of Benzonia, Michigan, from 1860 to 1890, Robert E. Bieder concluded that kinship ties with others in the community reduced emigration because economic opportunities not available to "outsiders"—such as the acquisition of land and entree into small businesses or industries—were open to extended family members. Although Onondaga townships did not have the intensive kinship structure Bieder found in Benzonia, his findings nonetheless are similar to what can be seen in the New York county.[10]

Since family relationships are difficult, if not impossible, to determine in a random sample of the population in 1830, the extent of kinship connections were estimated using the manuscript census schedules. All sample members who lived within five houses (as visited by the census taker) of another individual with the same last name were treated as living near relatives. In effect, this measure ignores family ties through the female line, where name changes would disguise the relationship between families, as well as extended families and relationships through the male line which happened to be beyond the five-house limit. Yet despite clearly underestimating family ties, the measure of kinship uncovered a surprisingly broad pattern of family relationships which survived over time.

Kin-as-neighbor relationships were most common in Manlius and had the greatest effect on migration and persistence there. More than one-quarter of all Manlius sample members lived within five houses of a relative through the male line in 1830. However only 23 percent of the migrants who left Manlius in the 1830s were living near kin at the beginning of the decade, while 30 percent of those who remained in the town at least until 1840 had been residing near other family members in 1830. This suggests that the presence of kin acted as a restraining force on emigration from Manlius in the 1830s. The importance of kinship-neighbor relationships to persistence is even more evident among sample members who remained in Manlius for twenty-five years or more. Fully 58.3 percent of these long-term persisters had been living near kinfolk in 1830. (See Table 6.7.)

The impact of kinship upon migration was apparently much less in Lysander and Fabius. Both townships had smaller proportions of their populations living near kin in 1830 (17 percent and 18

Table 6.7. **Kinship and Persistence**

	Migrants 1830s	Persisters 1840
Manlius		
Relatives nearby	23	30
No relatives nearby	77	70
Total	100	100
N	62	53
Fabius		
Relatives nearby	18	21
No relatives nearby	83	80
Total	101	101
N	63	39
Lysander		
Relatives nearby	18	16
No relatives nearby	82	84
Total	100	100
N	62	37

SOURCE: Sample data.

percent, respectively) than was true in Manlius. Residents of Fabius who persisted until 1840 were more likely to have had relatives nearby in 1830 than those who migrated, although the difference was considerably less than the difference between the two groups in Manlius. (See Table 6.7.) The situation was reversed, however, in Lysander where sample members who persisted until 1840 were slightly less likely to have had relatives in the township in 1830 than those who emigrated from Lysander in the 1830s. The discrepancies between the three townships suggest that where kin-as-neighbor relationships were widespread, they exerted social pressures against migration, pressures that were much weaker and more variable in townships with lower levels of kinship settlement.

Although both kinship and landownership influenced persistence in Manlius, the two factors together did not provide a stronger impetus to persistence than either alone. The percentage difference between landowners with kin and landowners without kin was only 1.6 while the percentage difference between landowners who lived near kin and landless residents living near kin was 2.1. The small size of the differences reflects the fact that individuals with land were not more likely to have nearby kin than others in the population. Moreover, in the township of Fabius, where kinship settlement patterns were less well developed than in Manlius, a higher proportion of the landless had local kinship ties than did the landowners (14 percent of the landowners and 24 percent of the landless had nearby relatives). The two variables were, in short, independent.

There was another side to family influences upon migration that may account for the reverse effect of kinship in Lysander and Manlius. Often migration of one family member led to the subsequent migration of others in the family, and many families separated by emigration were later reunited in the West. Although the extent of this pattern can not be computed from the samples of hinterland residents in 1830 because of the difficulties in obtaining data on kinship relations in places of western migration, some examples of this phenomenon are suggestive. Lucinda Fuller, a resident of Cicero, moved to Michigan soon after her marriage in 1836. She was visited from time to time by her family, and in 1853 her brother, William Eastwood, decided to move to Michigan after a visit to his sister. Equally common were instances in which elderly parents moved from Onondaga to Michigan, Ohio, or Illinois to live their last years with their children and their children's families. Typical of these older migrants were Enoch Ely and his wife, who sold the hotel they had managed in Fabius for forty years and moved to Michigan to live with their daughter.[11]

The Elys also illustrate a third influence upon migration from the Onondaga hinterland—age or stage of life. The impact of age on migration varied considerably in the period under study. The urge to migrate affected the young and the middle-aged more strongly than the rest of the sample members. In the 1830s, the heaviest migration from the three townships took place among sample members aged 20 to 29. These people generally had few economic assets and little personal investment in the county. Just as important, they could expect increasing needs and responsibilities over time; this, combined with the fact that their families were young and often still small, frequently led to the decision to emigrate. Of all sample members in this cohort in 1830, only 32 percent still resided in the township of enumeration in 1840. The highest persistence rates were found in the middle cohorts, ages 30 to 39 and 40 to 49, each of which had a 44 percent persistence rate for the decade, and in the oldest cohort of 60- to 69-year-olds, which had a persistence rate of 42 percent. (See Table 6.1.)

There were some changes in these tendencies in the 1840s. While most cohorts exhibited less out-migration than they had in the previous decade, the age group least likely to migrate in the 1830s, those over 60, actually increased its migration rate slightly between 1840 and 1850. In contrast with the pattern of the 1830s, persistence rates were high in the 1840s, with 73 percent of those who were between 30 and 39 in 1840 persisting until 1850. The estimated rate of migration in the 1840s, taking expected mortality into consideration, suggests that out-migration was most frequent in the 40 to 49 year cohort. (See Table 6.2.)

In addition, many older people like the Elys migrated from the Onondaga hinterland after long periods of residence in the county. It is difficult to determine exactly how many of the household heads over the age of 50 who disappeared from county records actually emigrated and how many died. However, more than one-third of all migrant sample members who can be traced to new locations outside the state of New York in this decade were over the age of 50 when they migrated. Ranging in age from 53 to 76, these sample members had lived in the county hinterland for varying periods of time, from twenty-six to sixty-two years, and left Onondaga County in their old age to be with distant family and friends. Had their children not left Onondaga, these individuals might have remained in the county where they had spent their lives, but ties with their families were stronger for these elderly migrants than were ties with a particular place. When Alexis de Tocqueville wrote that democracy not only makes "every man forget his ancestors, but it hides his descendants...and threatens in the end to confine him entirely within the solitude of his own heart," he was speaking of Americans in general. Yet if Onondaga County is at all typical (and the frequency of kinship-related settlement, persistence, and migration patterns would indicate that this was a widespread practice not confined to Onondaga), not even great geographical distances or many years' absence could keep nineteenth-century families apart.[12]

Ultimately, migration was related to economic conditions in the county hinterland as well as personal considerations such as stage of life or ties with relatives and friends. The rapid growth of the population of rural and village Onondaga, engendered by the optimism of the early settlement period and the initial response to the Erie Canal, overburdened the local economy, which was itself constricting even as the demands placed on it to absorb more workers were growing. Onondagans frequently responded to this situation by migrating. Although many residents moved short distances back and forth across the county hinterland or to adjacent counties before they settled "permanently," many others, including Onondagans who had lived in the county for a long time, went to the newly opened, cheap lands of the western states. They were impelled westward partly by the sheer availability of good transportation and anticipation of obtaining land, and partly by a cultural consensus that opportunity lay in the West.[13]

The city of Syracuse exerted far less influence upon hinterland migration during this period than its growing commercial importance might indicate. Migration to Syracuse from the hinterland was only a small part of the migration within and from the county and was largely confined to individuals whose training or capital gave them a competitive advantage in the city that most farmers lacked. For the heads of families in the hinterland, adults with responsibilities and often few financial assets, the opportunities in other rural and village locations were usually more attractive than the unfamiliar and demanding economic possibilities in the nearby city.

Notes

1. See Chapters 2 and 3 for a more complete description of these changes. See also Douglass C. North, *The Economic Growth of the United States, 1790-1860* (New York: W. W. Norton & Co., 1961), pp. 117-121.

2. See the Appendix for a discussion of the samples used in this analysis.

3. For information on geographical mobility in other regions, see Peter R. Knights, *The Plain People of Boston, 1830-1860: A Study in City Growth* (New York: Oxford University Press, 1971), pp. 103-118; Merle Curti, *The Making of an American Community: A Case Study of Democracy in a Frontier County* (Stanford, Calif.: Stanford University Press, 1959), pp. 55-83; Allan G. Bogue, *From Prairie to Corn Belt: Farming on the Illinois and Iowa Prairies in the Nineteenth Century* (Chicago: University of Chicago Press, 1963), pp. 8-28; and Mildred Throne, "A Population Study of an Iowa County in 1850," *Iowa Journal of History*, 42 (1959), 305-330.

4. Of those who migrated, 10 percent moved to other Onondaga locations. Mortality estimates were calculated from model life tables in Ansley J. Coale and Paul Demeny, *Regional Model Life Tables and Stable Populations* (Princeton: Princeton University Press, 1966), p. 15, according to the following formula:

$$1-\left(\frac{L(x+10)+L(x+15)}{L(x)+L(x+5)}\right)$$

See also Maris A. Vinovskis, "Mortality Rates and Trends in Massachusetts Before 1860," *Journal of Economic History*, 32 (March 1972), 184-213.

5. Since the mortality estimates apply to the entire group and cannot indicate which individuals actually died within each decade, the following discussion of migration is based upon the non-persisters of each decade, excluding those who are known to have died during the decade. See also Marcellus, New York, "Church Records from First Presbyterian, St. John's Episcopal and Methodist Churches," typescript at the Syracuse

Public Library; and George R. Smith, *A History of the First Eighty Years of the First Presbyterian Church of Marcellus, New York* (Canandaigua, N.Y.: Ontario County Times, 1883).

6. The migration figures of the Marcellus congregation probably underestimate the extent of out-migration from Onondaga County. Church members were undoubtedly more residentially stable by virtue of their institutional affiliation than a comparable group of the population chosen at random. Moreover, roughly two-thirds of all members were women. This unequal sex distribution skews the migration pattern, overestimating total migration to nearby locations and underestimating migration to the western states. Although many women migrated with their husbands, many others went alone. Single women have traditionally moved shorter distances than men, and among members of First Presbyterian Church, women moved within Onondaga County in greater proportions than men. For a discussion of sexual differences in migration patterns, see Pitirim Sorokin and Carle C. Zimmerman, *Principles of Rural-Urban Sociology* (New York: Henry Holt and Company, 1929), pp. 546-557; and Donald J. Bogue, *Principles of Demography* (New York: John Wiley & Sons, 1969), pp. 764-768.

7. Israel Parsons, *The Centennial History of the Town of Marcellus* (Marcellus, N.Y.: Reed's Printing House, 1878), pp. 71-73; Mrs. Will Bryum, "Early History of Onondaga," in Mrs. Franc L. Adams, ed., *Pioneer History of Ingham County* [*Michigan*], I (Lansing: Wynkoop Hallenbeck Crawford Company, 1923), pp. 681-714; Bruce, *Onondaga's Centennial*, I, pp. 225, 655; Noble E. Whitford, *History of the Canal System of the State of New York*, I, *Supplement to the Annual Report of the State Engineer and Surveyor of the State of New York, 1905* (Albany: Brandon Printing Co., 1906), p. 823.

8. Curti also found that large landowners were less likely to migrate than small landowners. See *The Making of an American Community*, pp. 55-83.

9. The mean size of persisters' farms is calculated only for those who actually owned farms in 1850.

10. Robert E. Bieder, "Kinship as a Factor in Migration," *Journal of Marriage and the Family,* 35 (August 1973), 429-439.

11. Asa Eastwood Papers, George Arents Research Library, Syracuse University. For other examples of both types of migration, see the family sketches in Bruce, *Onondaga's Centennial,* II; Heman Ely, compiler, *Records of the Descendents of Nathaniel Ely, the Emigrant, Who Settled First in Newtown, now Cambridge, Mass., was one of the first Settlers of*

Hartford, also of Norwalk Conn., and a Resident of Springfield, Mass., From 1659 until his death in 1675 (Cleveland: Short & Forman, Printers and Stationers, 1885).

12. Merle Curti found a similarly high migration or non-persistence rate for migrants over the age of 50 in nineteenth-century Trempealeau County, Wisconsin, which he attributes to higher death rates. See Curti, *The Making of an American Community*, p. 67. An examination of expected mortality for this age group, however, reveals that despite a higher mortality rate, the elderly sample members in Onondaga County were still migrating in large proportions. See also Alexis de Tocqueville, *Democracy in America,* II (New York: Vintage, 1945), pp. 104-106.

13. See Richard A. Easterlin, "Population Change and Farm Settlement in the Northern United States," *Journal of Economic History*, 36 (1976), 45-75.

CHAPTER 7

Conclusion

Between 1790 and 1860, the years during which Onondaga County was settled and the city of Syracuse was established, the population of the United States increased by 700 percent and its area by more than two million square miles. Equally important as the sheer increase in the size of the nation and its population was a change in the distribution of the people on the land. While only 5 percent of the population lived in cities in 1790, 20 percent—or one out of every five Americans—lived in cities in 1860. Yet despite the years of physical expansion and urban growth, the country's economy was more tightly knit than was true seventy years earlier, for changes in transportation brought the distant parts of the nation more closely together than had been possible when the physical distance between settlements had been shorter but more difficult to bridge.[1]

The cumulative effects of transportation changes and urban growth can be seen clearly in Onondaga County. In 1810, there was a distinct trading sector in Onondaga which lined either side of the Seneca Turnpike, the major highway between the settlements of eastern New York and the lands of the West. Within this sector there were numerous villages serving as commercial centers for local residents and transportation stations for passing travelers. There were also the salt springs villages lining Onondaga Lake and several agricultural settlements that were off the turnpike in well-settled farming areas. Local processing industries were scattered throughout the county, located where water power and trees were most abundant. County agriculture, dominated by grains and particularly by wheat, was similar throughout the county regardless of the varying quality of local soils.

The face of the county changed dramatically with the construction of the Erie Canal between 1820 and 1825. The central trading sector shifted northward from the turnpike to the canal, and settlements along the new waterway began to expand rapidly. The most important of these settlements was Syracuse, whose transportation advantages by 1830 included the Erie and Oswego Canals and a regional road system which converged upon the salt springs. By that year, moreover, county administrative offices had been moved to Syracuse and the village had become the interregional trading depot for both the county and the wider region of which the county was a part. The turnpike villages dwindled in importance, their populations declined, and many of their businessmen moved to Syracuse because of the economic opportunities the city offered.

The construction of several railroads between the 1830s and the 1850s further increased the importance of Syracuse as a transportation center and contributed to its continued rapid growth. Yet at the same time, population growth rates declined sharply in the county hinterland. In almost all hinterland townships, out-migrants exceeded in-migrants and the limited population increase that did occur was due to the high rate of natural increase. Out-migration took place largely from the rural areas and not from the villages. Hinterland farmers moved to better farming areas, often to the cheaper lands in the west or to local villages, while business and professional people and skilled workers migrated to the city of Syracuse.

The rural population exodus was partly due to the agricultural crisis that confronted Onondaga farmers in the late 1830s and throughout the 1840s. Because county agriculture was so dependent upon grains, soil exhaustion and crop-destroying insects rendered Onondaga farmers less able to compete with the products of western agriculture which, by the 1840s, were transported cheaply by canal to the same eastern markets long used by Onondaga farmers. In response to this crisis and to the growth of the Syracuse market, farmers began to put less of their land in grains for export and more into garden crops, fruit, potatoes, and dairy products. Some of these products were also shipped profitably to eastern cities by the railroad, which provided faster transportation for perishables than did the canal.

By the 1850s, economic activities in Onondaga were clearly segregated. The rural hinterland produced agricultural products. The villages of the hinterland provided limited commercial and industrial services, and the city dominated county commerce and non-agricultural industrial production and distribution, and controlled investment capital in the county. Syracuse had become the heart of the county in ways other than geographical. In addition to its position as a major agricultural market and a regional and interregional transportation center, it was also the commercial, legal, political, and social center of Onondaga County.

The experience of Onondaga County demonstrates how closely city-regions such as Syracuse were tied to the national economy in the nineteenth century. While exports were important, exports alone were not responsible for the development of the economy and the growth of the population in particular city-regions. Rather, regional growth was strongly influenced by national patterns of population growth and western migration which, together, created growing markets for agricultural products in both newly settled areas and eastern cities. National population movements also provided an essential external source of new residents for frontier cities and, to a lesser extent, their hinterlands. Transportation innovation and the extension of a national transportation network into newly settled areas directed these migrants to specific locations along well-traveled paths. More important, perhaps, interregional or national transportation systems improved the efficiency of existing market patterns and created new trading relationships within and between regions. As a result of interregional transportation improvements and the consequent marketing advantages they provided, certain settlements in developing areas became local or regional commercial centers as well as interregional transportation and trade centers.[2]

The resulting growth of these commercial cities encouraged greater specialization in the economic activities of their hinterlands and eventually transformed what had been a mixed rural economy into a specialized agricultural economy supported by occasional villages. The differentiation of Onondaga County into urban, rural, and village economies in the first half of the nineteenth century illustrates this process. As we have seen, the construction of the Erie Canal initiated the process through the introduction of new marketing efficiencies and the growth of the city of Syracuse. Economic activity, which had been relatively similar in all parts of the county before 1820 (except in those areas characterized by the exploitation of mineral resources), became increasingly specialized in the next several decades within particular urban, rural, or village locations.

The improvements in interregional transportation and communication provided by the canal system established a more efficient and a more stable economy based on a sharper segregation of economic functions within the country. However, the stimulus to this locational specialization of economic functions was not industrialization, as Eric E. Lampard has suggested, but rather the expansion of the existing national marketing system and the growth of a regional commercial network in the city-region.[3]

As the growing regional center for commerce and transportation, Syracuse possessed an important locational advantage by mid-century which the construction of both interregional and regional railroads could only enhance. Thus Allan Pred's description of the initial advantage existing commercial cities enjoyed during the rapid urbanization of the nineteenth century applies as well to this system of smaller frontier settlements for the period following the completion of the Erie Canal. Once the process of urban growth began, forces like the railroad, which might as easily have contributed to the growth of a different urban center, served instead to augment the growth of the existing city.[4]

Because Syracuse and its surrounding hinterland together formed but a single city-region, an examination of the patterns of change in Onondaga County between the time it was first settled and 1860 cannot by itself provide a theory of regional growth for developing areas. Yet the study of this small region in the nineteenth century can contribute to the accumulation of evidence necessary to build such a theory. Moreover, it suggests several ways in which our thinking about the growth of cities and the development of their hinterlands—urbanization in the broad sense—should be modified.

First, urban and regional development patterns in the nineteenth century were determined by the interplay between local conditions and the impact of forces located at the national and subnational levels. Too often local studies—or histories of single cities—focus on local developments, attributing the social and economic changes in a particular community solely to events within that community. Because this approach ignores important national and regional influences on urban development, it can only distort the history of the city. On the other hand, one of the rarely exploited advantages of case studies of single cities is that the local impact of national forces can be observed so clearly. For example, we have seen that the immediate impetus for the growth of Syracuse was the construction of a canal by the state of New York, which resulted in a reorientation and consolidation of both local and interregional marketing patterns. In addition, most of the city's population came from outside the the county hinterland and a large proportion from outside the United States. In short, the stimulus to the growth of Syracuse was not solely—or even predominantly—events or pressures (demographic or economic) within the region. The growth of the city was the result of a complex of national forces and local reactions to them.

Just as the city's growth was tied closely to actions in the larger society, the formation and development of what became the urban hinterland was interwoven with the growth of the city. We have seen that the city of Syracuse was enriched at the expense of the hinterland, particularly when the ablest people engaged in nonagricultural pursuits in the hinterland migrated to Syracuse or when hinterland investment capital was drawn to urban instead of hinterland investments. Eventually, however, the growing population in the city provided an invaluable market for hinterland agriculture, which had suffered a competitive disadvantage from the opening of western areas to the national grain markets.

Examining national, regional, or local trends alone will not reveal this interaction nor will it show differences between what was taking place at the national and the local levels. For instance, data on national population growth in the middle of the nineteenth century, if unexamined, can mask the population decline in the agricultural hinterland of Syracuse. Similarly, the growth of the population of Onondaga County encompasses both rapid urban population growth and a declining rate of growth in the city's hinterland.

Second, the study of Syracuse and its hinterland shows the importance of interregional transportation improvements to regional development. While transportation improvements were generally introduced to facilitate interregional trade (and usually accomplished that purpose), their role in the subsequent formation of a regional economy is less widely recognized. Since the time von Thünen created his isolated state and described its growth, development theorists have frequently viewed regional development as a stage in the formation of a national economy. According to this view, an initial subsistence village economy is succeeded by a period of regional development, characterized by improvements in regional transportation, the beginnings of regional trade, and the growth of small industry for local consumption. This, in turn, is followed by a period of regional specialization and interregional trade.[5]

Whatever the applicability of this model to regional development in Europe, where it originated, it fails to describe what took place in North America. As the experience of Syracuse and Onondaga County illustrates, transportation innovations and regional development in the United States occurred within the framework of an existing national economy. Before the construction of the canal, commercial and other economic contacts between the frontier area and eastern settlements were extensive and diffuse, making areas like Onondaga County part of the east coast, or national, economy from the time they were first settled. Transportation improvements, in this case the Erie Canal, promoted the formation of a regional marketing system which fed local trade more efficiently into existing national markets. The new regional trading patterns were funneled through Syracuse, replacing what had been the dispersed individualized marketing patterns of county residents.

Evidence can be found of the importance of transportation innovations in the development of other city-regions as well. Stuart Blumin notes that after a canal was built to the Hudson River at Kingston, New York, the town, though never isolated, became more closely tied to the national market in New York City than it had been, and at the same time became more important as a regional and local commercial center. At quite a different scale, Bessie L. Pierce showed that the construction of the railroads in the 1850s turned Chicago, which had been an interregional trading center, into a regional center as well. Similarly, Edward K. Muller describes a "concentration of commerce" which took place in the middle Ohio Valley in the late 1820s after the opening of the Miami Canal. Local trade was attracted to those towns and villages on the canal that had access to larger markets elsewhere.[6]

A third conclusion which can be drawn from the experience of Syracuse and Onondaga County is that urban growth did not benefit all parts of the city-region equally. Today the mixed blessings of urban growth are increasingly apparent as sprawling land use patterns and industrial, automotive, and household pollution affect city and hinterland alike. However even in the nineteenth century, when growth was more directly related in the public mind to progress and prosperity, urban growth had unfortunate consequences for the city's hinterland. As we have seen, the growing city of Syracuse absorbed many of the political, economic, and, eventually, the social functions of nearby villages and thus hindered their growth. This was accompanied by a drain of hinterland residents with skills, training, and investment capital to the city.

There has been little previous examination of the effects of urban growth on the surrounding hinterland. Notable exceptions are the work of James T. Lemon and Michael Conzen. Examining southeastern Pennsylvania in the eighteenth century, Lemon found that the city of Philadelphia dominated its immediate hinterland as Syracuse dominated Onondaga County. Its impact, however, was much greater and towns within a thirty-mile radius of Philadelphia did not grow at all. Conzen studied a much smaller area, Blooming Grove township outside Madison, Wisconsin, in the nineteenth century. The township had no settlements, but Conzen found that the presence of the city affected the initial disposition of the agricultural land and subsequent patterns of land use. Land values near the city were high, and Conzen speculates that this was responsible for higher levels of tenancy in Blooming Grove than in areas farther from the city. Much later, of course, suburban expansion radically changed the pattern of land use in Blooming Grove.[7]

Clearly, more research is needed in this area. The conditions under which settlement took place in Onondaga County and both Blooming Grove township and southeastern Pennsylvania were quite different. Onondaga County was settled before the city of

Syracuse appeared, but Blooming Grove and the area around Philadelphia were always, as Conzen terms it, in an urban shadow. Depite these differences, the fact that the growth of these cities was so influential in the development of their hinterlands suggests that the effect of urban growth on nonurban areas is a subject deserving greater attention than it has previously received.

Another subject that needs to be investigated further is the etiology of regional growth in the nineteenth century. This study shows what happened in one New York county located along the path of interregional transportation systems, but development patterns undoubtedly differed in areas located at some distance from the major transportation routes. The changes which took place in southern Onondaga County in the 1850s after the Syracuse and Binghamton Railroad was constructed suggest that similar social and economic changes took place whenever interregional transportation improvements were first introduced to a settled area. Yet interregional transportation systems were not extended to some parts of the settled United States during the nineteenth century. Where they were constructed, moreover, they may have played a different role in regional development than they did in Onondaga County. For example, interregional transportation systems in the western states often accompanied or even preceded initial settlement and consequently their impact on subsequent settlement and marketing patterns undoubtedly differed. An examination of city-regions in other sections of the United States and over other periods of time would indicate how the timing and the technology of interregional transportation systems influenced social and economic development. The experience of Onondaga County may simply be illustrative of city-regions which were settled or underwent a period of rapid growth in the first half of the nineteenth century, while other city-regions, settled later or earlier under different conditions, may have experienced quite different patterns of growth and development.

This study of Onondaga County also underlines our lack of knowledge of the process of migration in the nineteenth century. Too little is known about the relationship between sending and receiving areas. The evidence in Onondaga County suggests that American migrants often retained closed social and economic ties with their homes of origin, just as, years later, they remained close to their grown children who had migrated still farther west.

More should also be learned about the impact of national migration patterns on local settlement patterns and about the factors that influence migration to a particular place. There were several different migration streams into and out of Onondaga County in the nineteenth century. The pioneer farmer, though he captured the imaginations of several generations, was illustrative of only one of these migration streams. Local migrants, who moved from place to place within a small geographical area, urban migrants, who moved from rural areas to the fast-growing cities, and city-hoppers were also found in nineteenth-century Onondaga and, very likely, in other parts of the United States as well.

But the story of Syracuse and Onondaga County during this period of transportation change and rapid urban growth offers more than simple suggestions for further research. It shows how urbanization transformed the county. The rural area shaded over time into a growing city and its hinterland, until by 1860, the county bore little resemblance to the land of the Onondaga where Ephram Webster first went to trade so many years earlier.

Notes

1. U.S. Bureau of the Census, *Historical Statistics of the United States, Colonial Times to 1970, Bicentennial Edition, Part 1* (Washington: U.S. Government Printing Office, 1975), pp. 8-12.

2. See Douglass C. North, "Location Theory and Regional Economic Growth," *Journal of Political Economy*, 63 (1955), 243-258, for a discussion of the role of exports in the growth of regional economies.

3. Eric E. Lampard, "The History of Cities in the Economically Advanced Areas," *Economic Development and Cultural Change*, 3 (1955), 81-136.

4. Allan R. Pred, *The Spacial Dynamics of U.S. Urban-Industrial Growth, 1800-1914: Interpretive and Theoretical Essays* (Cambridge: M.I.T. Press, 1966), pp. 143-215.

5. Johann Heinrich von Thünen, *The Isolated State*, translated by Carla M. Wartenberg and edited with an introduction by Peter Hall (Oxford and London: Pergamon Press, 1966).

6. Stuart M. Blumin, *The Urban Threshold: Growth and Change in a Nineteenth-Century Community* (Chicago: University of Chicago Press,

1976), p. 63; Bessie L. Pierce, *A History of Chicago, Volume II: From Town to City, 1848-1871* (New York: Alfred A. Knopf, 1940), pp. 3-4, 39, and 106; and Edward K. Muller, "Selective Urban Growth in the Middle Ohio Valley, 1800-1860," *The Geographical Review*, 66 (1976), 178-199.

7. James T. Lemon, *The Best Poor Man's Country: A Geographical Study of Early Southeastern Pennsylvania* (Baltimore: Johns Hopkins University Press, 1972), pp. 130-131; and Michael P. Conzen, *Frontier Farming in An Urban Shadow* (Madison: State Historical Society of Wisconsin, 1971).

APPENDIX

The samples used to analyze persistence and migration patterns in the county hinterland consist of independent systematic samples of household heads in Lysander, Manlius, and Fabius. One in five heads of household in Lysander and Fabius, towns with totals of 510 and 518 heads of household, were chosen for the sample. There were 1,220 heads of household in Manlius—more than twice as many as in Lysander and Fabius. Consequently, one of every ten heads of household was included in the sample.

Of necessity, all 326 sample members are heads of households, for not until 1850 did the federal census record the names of household members other than the head. Peter Knights (in a report of the Eastern Historical Geographers Association meeting in Boston, November 3-4, 1972, published in *Historical Methods Newsletter*, 6 [December 1972], 36-37) suggests that the historian use vital statistics, city directories, and tax records in preference to the manuscript census returns. However, of the three, only tax records of landowners are available for Onondaga residents in the years prior to 1860—and these can only be found for certain towns. City directories did not extend to rural areas or villages, and even population listings which might provide the basis for a sample, such as the tax rolls or church membership lists, were biased to exclude sizable portions of the population, such as the landless and non-church members. Although scholars are becoming increasingly aware of the difficulties in relying solely upon census records in describing sample populations, the manuscript census remains, nonetheless, the best place to begin a population study of early nineteenth-century America.

Although the federal census reports provided the most complete listing from which to choose a sample, they were only the beginning of the information that could be assembled on the sample members. Information on individuals was available in the extensive genealogical records on former Onondaga County residents, in records of land transactions, which give the residences of those who sold and those who purchased the land, in church and burial ground records, and membership lists of voluntary organizations, in addition to earlier and subsequent state and federal censuses. A surprisingly fruitful source of information about migration, genealogical research supplied the destinations of many out-of-state emigrants and often suggested the motivation for such migration. There were, to be sure, difficulties as well. Both the census taker and the genealogist frequently ignored or simply missed transient individuals. Moreover, these frequent migrants rarely owned land and thus left no legal records in the county court house. However by restricting the samples to household heads, we are restricting it to the most visible portion of a broad cross-section of the community. Genealogical records were available at the Syracuse Public Library and the Onondaga Historical Association in Syracuse. The Pioneer File of Onondaga residents prior to 1850 at the Syracuse Public Library was also helpful. An index to existing genealogical records, it directed me to published and unpublished documents for each individual in the file.

The samples are not confined to male heads of household. Although women have been traditionally harder to trace through conventional sources, such as city directories, tax assessments, and census schedules, this is not the case in genealogical and land records. Genealogists are as eager for information about their female ancestors as they are about those who were male, and women can usually be found under both their married and their maiden names. Moreover, although most land purchases were made by men, all land sales were registered under the names of both husband and wife, so that the transactions of widows prior to their widowhood and those of women who subsequently married can be traced as easily as those of men or of women who never married. Although the proportion of female household heads on whom we have no information from any source is slightly higher than the proportion of males in the same category, the elimination of women from the samples would result in an unnecessary loss of approximately 5 percent of the combined samples and cause a serious distortion in the collective portrait of migration in Onondaga County. Although no information beyond the census listing was found on 20 percent of the female heads of household, this was only 4 percent higher than the 16 percent of male heads of household who were not traceable beyond the 1830 manuscript schedules of the federal census.

BIBLIOGRAPHIC ESSAY

The following is an abbreviated bibliography of the most important items consulted on the development of Onondaga County. For a fuller description of materials used in this study, consult the notes to each chapter.

Transportation Studies

The best general accounts of transportation changes during the antebellum period are George Rogers Taylor, *The Transportation Revolution* (New York: Holt, Rinehart and Winston, 1951) and the essays in Caroline E. MacGill et al., *History of Transportation in the United States before 1860* (Washington: Carnegie Institute of Washington, 1917). Taylor's work recently has been assessed in Harry N. Scheiber and Stephen Salsbury, "Reflections on George Rogers Taylor's *The Transportation Revolution, 1815-1860:* A Twenty-five Year Retrospect," *Business History Review* 51 (1977), 79-89. Directly focused on transportation in the state of New York is Col. William A. Bird, *New York State Early Transportation, Publications of the Buffalo Historical Society*, Vol. II (Buffalo: Bigelow Brothers, 1880). Bird deals extensively with transportation routes before the construction of the Erie Canal, as does Nathan Miller in *The Enterprise of a Free People: Aspects of Economic Development in New York State during the Canal Period, 1792-1838* (Ithaca: Cornell University Press, 1962). A first-hand description of transportation in Onondaga County in 1810 can be found in William W. Campbell, *The Life and Writings of DeWitt Clinton* (New York: Baker and Scribner, 1849). A description of chartered public roads and turnpikes is available in the New York State Divisional Engineer's Office, Third District. A typescript of these records is in the Onondaga Historical Association.

The most useful source of information on the Erie and Oswego Canals is the *Annual Reports of the Canal Commissioners.* The volume of canal traffic can be determined from the yearly *Reports of the Auditor of the Canal Department of the Tolls, Trade and Tonnage of the Canals*. See also the *Laws of the State of New York, in relation to the Erie and Champlain Canals, together with the annual reports of the canal commissioners and other documents,* 2 vols. (Albany: E. and E. Hosfor, 1825). Recognition of the city-building role of the canal appeared in Blake McKelvey, "The Erie Canal, Mother of Cities," *The New-York Historical Quarterly*, 35 (1951), 55-71. Its impact upon the distribution of capital in western New York is ably described by Nathan Miller in *Enterprise of a Free People,* while Lois Kimball Mathews deals with the importance of the canal in population movements in "The Erie Canal and the Settlement of the West," *Buffalo Historical Society Publications*, 14 (1910), 187-203. A parallel to the New York canal system can be seen in Harry N. Scheiber, *Ohio Canal Era: A Case Study of Government and the Economy, 1820-1861* (Athens: Ohio University Press, 1969).

The importance of the Erie Canal to the development of western New York state was stressed in 1900 by Julius Winden in "The Influence of the Erie Canal upon the Population Along Its Course" (B.Ph. thesis, University of Wisconsin, 1900). Noble E. Whitford's study, *History of the Canal System of the State of New York,* 2 vols., *Supplement to the Annual Report of the State Engineer and Surveyor of the State of New York, 1905* (Albany: Brandow Printing Company, 1906), used the same analysis to show the importance of the canal to the development of the entire region. Winden's work, through Whitford's adaptation, has been the standard interpretation of the role of the Erie Canal in New York since 1906. Most recently the same arguments have been reiterated by Ronald E. Shaw in *Erie Water West: A History of the Erie Canal, 1792-1854* (Lexington: University of Kentucky Press, 1966). For a discussion of the economic impact of canal construction, see Harvey H. Segal, "Canals and Economic Development," in Carter Goodrich, ed., *Canals and American Economic Development* (Port Washington, N.Y.: Kennikat Press, 1972 [reissue]), pp. 216-248. For a study of the implications of canal construction on a small town, see Stuart M. Blumin, *The Urban Threshold: Growth and Change in a Nineteenth-Century Community* (Chicago: University of Chicago Press, 1976).

For a discussion of the role of the canal in the growth of manufacturing between 1820 and 1840, see Roger L. Ransom, "Interregional Canals and Economic Specialization in the Antebellum United States," *Explorations in Entrepreneurial History*, 2nd Ser., 5 (1967), 12-35; Albert W. Niemi, Jr., "A Further Look at Interregional Canals and Western Manufacturing," *Explorations in Entrepreneurial History*, 2nd Ser., 7(1970), 499-520; and Ransom, "A Closer Look at Canals and Western Manufacturing,"

Explorations in Entrepreneurial History, 2nd Ser., 8 (1971), 501-508. Edward K. Muller deals with transportation, urban growth, and manufacturing in "Selective Urban Growth in the Middle Ohio Valley, 1800-1860," *The Geographical Review,* 66 (1976), 178-199.

The advent of the railroads in Onondaga County can be followed in the pages of the *American Railroad Journal* and *Advocate of Internal Improvements.* Fred Walker Stevens, *The Beginnings of the New York Central Railroad* (New York: G. P. Putnam's Sons, 1926), gives descriptions of the railroads which later were merged into the New York Central Railroad, and Lewis H. Haney, *A Congressional History of Railways in the United States,* Vol. I (Madison: Democratic Printing Co., State Printer, 1908), discusses debates over the relative advantages of canals and railroads. This rivalry is also the subject of an article by David Maldwyn Ellis, "Rivalry between the New York Central and the Erie Canal," *New York History*, 14 (1948), 268-300. See also William C. Redfield, *Sketch of the Geographical Rout of a Great Railway*. Second ed. (New-York: G. & C. & H. Carvill, 1830). The impact of railroads on the national economy is the subject of Robert W. Fogel, *Railroads and American Economic Growth* (Baltimore: Johns Hopkins University Press, 1964), and Albert Fishlow, *American Railroads and the Transformation of the Antebellum Economy* (Cambridge: Harvard University Press, 1965).

Agriculture, Commerce, and Industry

The best general introduction to agriculture during this period is Clarence H. Danhof, *Change in Agriculture: The Northern United States, 1820-1870* (Cambridge: Harvard University Press, 1969). Percy Wells Bidwell and John I. Falconer, *History of Agriculture in the Northern United States, 1620-1860*, Carnegie Institution of Washington, Publication No. 358 (New York: Peter Smith, 1941), is also valuable, as is Paul W. Gates, *The Farmer's Age: Agriculture, 1815-1860* (New York: Holt, Rinehart and Winston, 1960). Russell H. Anderson, "New York Agriculture Meets the West, 1830-1850," *Wisconsin Magazine of History*, 16 (1932-1933), offers a more specific analysis of agriculture in central and western New York and its competition with the new farms in the Northwest.

Nineteenth-century commercial activities are described in Glenn Porter and Harold C. Livesay, *Merchants and Manufacturers: Studies in the Changing Structure of Nineteenth-Century Marketing* (Baltimore: Johns Hopkins University Press, 1971) and in their article, "Financial Role of Merchants in the Development of U.S. Manufacturing, 1815-1860," *Explorations in Economic History,* 2nd Series, 9 (1971), 63-88. Also helpful was Fred Mitchell Jones, *Middlemen in the Domestic Trade of the*

United States, 1800-1860 (Urbana: University of Illinois Press, 1937). Less useful was Carol Halpert Schwartz, "Retail Trade Development in New York State in the Nineteenth Century with Special Reference to the Country Store" (Ph.D. dissertation, Columbia University, 1963). National business conditions during the antebellum period were described by Walter Buckingham Smith and Arthur Harrison Cole, *Wholesale Commodity Prices in the United States, 1700-1861,* 2 vols. (Cambridge: Harvard University Press, 1938), and in Thomas Senior Berry, *Western Prices Before 1861: A Study of the Cincinnati Market* (Cambridge: Harvard University Press, 1943). Information on the activities of a major railroad and on banking in the entire region of central New York was found in Irene D. Neu, *Erastus Corning, Merchant and Financier, 1794-1872* (Ithaca: Cornell University Press, 1960). Robert W. Silsby, "Frontier Attitudes and Debt Collection in Western New York," in David M. Ellis, ed., *The Frontier in American Economic Development: Essays in Honor of Paul Wallace Gates* (Ithaca: Cornell University Press, 1969), provided an understanding of the rapid changes of ownership in Onondaga County businesses.

Interregional trade is ably described in Robert G. Albion, *The Rise of New York Port, 1815-1860* (New York: Charles Scribner's Sons, 1939). Also helpful were Marvin A. Rapp, "New York's Trade on the Great Lakes, 1800-1840," *New York History*, 39 (1958), 22-33, and Chilton Williamson, "New York's Impact on the Canadian Economy Prior to the Completion of the Erie Canal," *New York History*, 24 (1943), 24-38.

The fullest account of manufacturing in this period is in Victor S. Clark, *History of Manufactures in the United States,* Vol. I, 1607-1860 (Washington: Carnegie Institution of Washington, 1929). Invaluable for a study of home manufacture is Rolla Milton Tryon, *Household Manufactures in the United States 1640-1860: A Study in Industrial History* (Chicago: University of Chicago Press, 1917). Arthur Harrison Cole discusses both sheep raising and wool manufacture in *The American Wool Manufacture*, 2 vols. (Cambridge: Harvard University Press, 1926). Allan Pred discusses urban manufacturing in "Manufacturing in the American Mercantile City: 1800-1840," *The Spacial Dynamics of U.S. Urban-Industrial Growth, 1800-1914: Interpretive and Theoretical Essays* (Cambridge: M.I.T. Press, 1966). Peter Temin describes the use of steam and water power in "Steam and Waterpower in the Early Nineteenth Century," *Journal of Economic History,* 26 (1966), 187-205. Richard L. Ehrlich has discussed manufacturing in Onondaga County, focusing particularly on the salt industry, in "The Development of Manufacturing in Selected Counties in the Erie Canal Corridor, 1815-1860" (Ph.D. dissertation, State University of New York at Buffalo, 1972). Rural industry is described in Margaret Walsh, *The Manufacturing Frontier* (Madison: State Historical Society of Wisconsin, 1972).

Melvin L. Greenhut, *Plant Location in Theory and Practice: The Economics of Space* (Chapel Hill: University of North Carolina Press, 1956), discusses the non-economic factors that affect industrial location.

Migration

The settlement of Onondaga County was part of the westward movement described by Dixon Ryan Fox, *Yankees and Yorkers* (New York: New York University Press, 1940) and David M. Ellis, "The Yankee Invasion of New York, 1783-1850," *New York History*, 32 (1951), 3-17. Migration from New England is treated by Lois Kimball Mathews, *The Expansion of New England: The Spread of New England Settlement and Institutions to the Mississippi River, 1620-1865* (New York: Russell & Russell, 1962, originally published 1909). Mathews treats Azariah Smith, a Manlius settler, at great length. A superior account of a smaller migrant group is Lewis D. Stilwell, *Migration from Vermont 1776-1860,* Proceedings of the Vermont Historical Society, 1937, New Series, 5, No. 2. Mary Josephine Hasbrouck treats migration into Onondaga County in a paper delivered to the Onondaga Historical Association on March 11, 1938, "Why Early Settlers Came to Onondaga County" (typescript, Syracuse Public Library). A number of the early residents of the county came from Middlefield, Massachusetts; their migrations and family connections are described in Edward Church Smith and Phillip Mack Smith, *A History of the Town of Middlefield, Massachusetts* (Menasha, Wis.: The Collegiate Press, 1924) and Smith and Smith, *The Ancestors and Descendants of Samuel Smith, Senior, of Middlefield, Massachusetts* (typescript, Western Reserve Historical Society, Cleveland, Ohio). Migration out of the county was traced with the aid of innumerable genealogies, census manuscripts, and tax rolls, and the Pioneer File of the Syracuse Public Library, an alphabetical index to printed information on Onondaga County residents before 1850.

For a discussion of migration patterns in the nineteenth century, see Allan Pred, *The External Relations of Cities during 'Industrial Revolution' with a Case Study of Göteborg, Sweden: 1868-1890*, Chicago University Department of Geography, Research Paper No. 76 (Chicago: University of Chicago Press, 1962). John Modell discusses rural-to-urban migration at midcentury in "The Peopling of a Working-Class Ward: Reading, Pennsylvania, 1850," *Journal of Social History*, 5 (1971), 71-95, and Stephen Thernstrom discusses the migration of the urban working class in *Poverty and Progress: Social Mobility in a Nineteenth Century City* (Cambridge: Harvard University Press, 1964).

Local Histories

General histories of New York which proved helpful include David M. Ellis, James A. Frost, Harold C. Syrett, and Harry J. Carman, *A History of New York State* (Ithaca: Cornell University Press, 1957, 1967), and Freeman Galpin, *Central New York: An Inland Empire*, 4 vols. (New York: Lewis Historical Publishing Company, Inc., 1941). Indian villages and road systems prior to the arrival of white Americans were located in Lewis Henry Morgan, *League of the Ho-De-No Sau-Nee or Iroquois* (originally published New York: Dodd Mead & Co., 1901; reprinted in 2 volumes, New Haven: Human Relations Area Files, 1954).

Dwight H. Bruce, *Onondaga's Centennial: Gleanings of a Century*, 2 vols. ([Boston]: The Boston History Company, 1896), was the most inclusive history of Onondaga County. Despite its rambling style and occasional inaccuracies, this book was invaluable for preserving a broad range of materials pertaining to the early history of the county and its inhabitants. An important contemporary history was written by Joshua V.H. Clark, *Onondaga; or Reminiscences of Earlier and Later Times,* 2 vols. (Syracuse: Stoddard and Babcock, 1849); and somewhat later was W. W. Clayton, *History of Onondaga County, New York* (Syracuse: Mason & Co., 1878). See also Carroll E. Smith, *Pioneer Times in the Onondaga County* (Syracuse: E. W. Bardeen, 1904), and William Martin Beauchamp, *Past and Present of Syracuse and Onondaga County New York from Prehistoric Times to the Beginning of 1908*, 2 vols. (New York and Chicago: S. J. Clark Publishing Co., 1908). Eric Henry Faigle, *Syracuse: A Study in Urban Geography* (Ph.D. dissertation, University of Michigan, 1936), contained valuable maps of Syracuse and central Onondaga County.

The most useful of the town and village histories were Dwight H. Bruce, *Memorial History of Syracuse, New York, From Its Settlement to the Present Time* (Syracuse: H. P. Smith & Co., 1891); Franklin Chase, *Syracuse and Its Environs,* 3 vols. (New York: Lewis Historical Publishing Company, Inc., 1924); Louis Dow Scisco, *Early History of the Town of Van Buren, Onondaga County, New York* (Baldwinsville, N.Y.: W.F. Morris Publishing Company, 1895); Israel Parsons, *The Centennial History of the Town of Marcellus* (Marcellus, N.Y.: Reed's Printing House, 1878); and Edmund Norman Leslie, *Skaneateles: History of Its Earliest Settlement and Reminiscences of Later Times* (New York: Andrew H. Kellogg, 1902). Particularly valuable was the brief *History of Manlius Village* by Henry C. Van Schaack (Fayetteville, N.Y.: The Recorder Office, 1873). Van Schaack moved to Manlius in 1827 when he was 24 years of age, and most of what he reports from the early years of the town were places and events he remembered from his youth.

Other local histories which proved helpful were: Mary Ellis Maxwell, *Among the Hills of Camillus* (n.p.: 1952); William P. H. Hewitt, *History of the Diocese of Syracuse* (Syracuse: Catholic Sun Press, 1909); William Martin Beauchamp, ed., *Annual Volume of the Onondaga Historical Association* (Syracuse: Dehler Press, 1914); Carol Gossner, ed., *Fabius in History* (n.p.: 1938-39); L. Pearl Palmer, "Historical Review of the Town of Lysander" (series of articles from the *Baldwinsville Messenger*, 1941-1946); Lena Putnam Anguish, *History of Fayetteville-Manlius Area* (Manlius, N.Y.: Fayetteville-Manlius Central School District, 1966); Harry C. Durston, *History of Manlius, N.Y.* (Manlius, N.Y.: Eagle-Bulletin, 1935-1938); Rev. George R. Smith, *A History of the First Eighty Years of the First Presbyterian Church of Marcellus, N.Y.* (Canandaigua, N.Y.: Ontario County Times, 1883); Lester G. Wells, *The Skaneateles Communal Experiment, 1843-1846* (Syracuse: Onondaga Historical Association, 1953); Richard F. Palmer, "The Skaneateles Railroad" (typescript, 1965, Syracuse Public Library,); George Knapp Collins, *Spafford, Onondaga County, New York* (Syracuse: Dehler Press, 1917); W. Freeman Galpin, "The Genesis of Syracuse," *New York History*, 30 (1949), 19-32; M. C. Hand, *From a Forest to a City: Personal Reminiscences of Syracuse, N.Y.* (Syracuse: Masters and Stone, 1889).

Blake McKelvey's studies of the city of Rochester, particularly *Rochester: The Water-Power City, 1812-1854* (Cambridge: Harvard University Press, 1945), were valuable for comparing Syracuse with another canal city. Also important because of its regional emphasis was Whitney R. Cross, "Creating a City: Rochester, 1824-1834" (M.A. thesis, University of Rochester, 1936). H.C. Goodwin, *Pioneer History; or, Cortland County and the Border Wars of New York* (New York: A. B. Burdick, 1859), was helpful for information about neighboring Cortland County.

Printed Primary Sources

Travelers' accounts provided descriptions of early Onondaga, including Horatio Gates Spafford, *A Pocket Guide for the Tourist and Traveler along the lines of the Canals and the Interior Commerce of the State of New York* (New-York: T. & J. Swords, 1824); Christian Schultz, *Travels on an Inland Voyage through the States of New-York, Pennsylvania, Virginia, Ohio, Kentucky, and Tennessee, and through the Territories of Indiana, Louisiana, Mississippi and New Orleans; performed in the years 1807 and 1808* (New-York: I. Riley, 1810); Zerah Hawley, *A Journal of a Tour Through Connecticut, Massachusetts, New-York . . .* (New Haven: S. Converse, 1822); John Fowler, *Journal of a Tour in the State of New*

York, in the Year 1830 (London: Whittaker, Treacher, and Arnot, 1831); and Robert J. Vandervater, *The Tourist, or Pocket Manual for Travellers...* 3rd ed. (New York: Harper and Brothers, 1834). Benjamin DeWitt describes the very early years of Onondaga industry in *Memoir on the Onondaga Salt Springs and Salt Manufactories in the Western Part of the State of New-York* (Albany: Loring Andrews, 1798).

Also helpful were the descriptive gazetteers which abounded in this period. The earliest were the two by Horatio Gates Spafford, *A Gazetteer of the State of New York* (Albany: H. C. Southwick, 1813, and Albany: B. D. Packard, 1824). Thomas F. Gordon, *Gazetteer of the State of New York* (Philadelphia: printed for the author, 1836), published a valuable compendium for the 1830s; and in 1842, John Disturnell published a *Gazetteer of the State of New York* (Albany: John Disturnell, 1842) which provided more detailed information on villages. Useful guides to the end of the antebellum period are J. H. French, *Gazetteer of the State of New York* (Syracuse: R. P. Smith, 1860), and John W. Barber, *Historical Collections of the State of New York* (New York: Clark, Austin & Company, 1851). See also Sterling Goodenow, *A Brief Topographical and Statistical Manual of the State of New-York*, second ed. (New York: E. Bliss and E. White, 1822).

Helpful periodicals were *Hunt's Merchants' Magazine* (also called the *Merchants' Magazine & Commercial Review*), 1839-1860; *Transactions of the New York State Agricultural Society,* 1841-1865; and the aforementioned *American Railroad Journal* [*and Advocate of Internal Improvements*]. Particularly valuable were studies by Willis Gaylord, "Agriculture of Onondaga County," in the *Transactions of the New-York State Agricultural Society,* II (1843), pp. 174-186, and George Geddes, *Report on the Agriculture and Industry of the County of Onondaga, State of New York* (Albany: Charles Van Benthusyen, 1860).

An excellent collection of letters from Azariah and Joseph Smith to their parents in Massachusetts was reprinted by Albert V. House, Jr., in "Two Yankee Traders in New York: Letters on the Financing of Frontier Merchants, 1808-1830," *New England Quarterly*, 11 (1938), 607-631. Thurlow Weed, a resident of Onondaga County in his childhood and early adulthood, describes his experiences in the *Life of Thurlow Weed, including his Autobiography and a Memoir*, 2 vols. (Boston and New York: Houghton, Mifflin and Company, 1883-1884). Early salt making and shipping patterns are detailed in Lewis C. Beck, *An Account of the Salt Springs at Salina in Onondaga County, State of New-York* (New York: J. Seymour, 1826); and John Dobbins, *The Dobbins Papers, Publications of the Buffalo Historical Society,* 8 (1905), 257-379. Dobbins uses the papers of his father, a skipper on the Great Lakes in the early nineteenth century, in his account.

Various printed collections of church and school records were also helpful. These include James H. Hotchkin, *A History of the Purchase and Settlement of Western New York and of the Rise, Progress and Present State of the Presbyterian Church in that Section* (New York: M. W. Dodd, 1848); and A. Judd Northrup, ed., *Early Records of the First Presbyterian Church of Syracuse, N. Y.* (Syracuse: Genealogical Society of Central New York, 1902). Valuable school catalogues were the *Catalogue of the Officers and Students of the Manlius Academy, Manlius, New York* (Manlius: C. W. Mason, 1835); *Catalogue of the Teachers and Students of Park Institute (Lake Cottage Seminary) for the Year ending November 19, 1852* (Syracuse: Truairs Print, n.d. [probably 1852 or 1853]); and *Catalogue of the Officers and Students of Pompey Academy, for the Year ending August 4, 1853* (Syracuse: Synkoop & Brother, 1853). Also useful were the various city directories for Syracuse that were issued after 1851.

Unpublished Materials

An important source of information was the Asa Eastwood collection at the George Arents Research Library, Syracuse University. The papers include a diary kept by Eastwood, a resident of Cicero, from before 1820 to the late 1860s. Similarly helpful, although it covered a shorter period of time, was the William B. Harris Journal (Department of Manuscripts and University Archives, Cornell University). Other manuscript collections consulted were the Wells Family Letters and Papers (Syracuse Public Library); the Green Family Papers, 1774-1889 (George Arents Research Library, Syracuse University); the White Family Papers, 1820-1937, the Collins Family Papers, 1841-1939, and the Berry Collection, 1812-1917, all at the Department of Manuscripts and University Archives, Cornell University.

A very short history of Manlius with rare village population statistics by age and sex for 1830 and 1840 has been preserved in typescript at the Syracuse Public Library. It was probably written by Joseph Smith, the brother of Azariah Smith, in the late 1840s. Erasmus Carr, "Remarks concerning the early history of the township of Tully, N.Y., 29 July, 1910" is also preserved at the Syracuse Public Library, as is an essay on "John Meeker, 1767-1840," by Herbert Barber Howe, a regional historian. Mary Munro has written "A Quarter Century with a Central New York Farmer, 1846-1871," from the diaries of John Munro, a resident of Elbridge (typescript, Syracuse Public Library).

A number of account books and ledgers proved to be helpful in determining the nature of village commerce. At the Onondaga Historical Association, the day books of the general store of Bissell and Pomeroy, 1838-1843, in Otisco and Amber, New York, and the Invoice Book of Oren

Tyler, 1822-1832, of Onondaga Hollow, provided some helpful information. There were a number of business records at the Department of Manuscripts and University Archives, Cornell University, including Rhodes and Company, Marcellus, New York, ledger, 1825-1830; letter and accounts for the Dexter and Northrup and the Dexter and Moseley stores in Salina in the Simon Newton Dexter Collection; Henry A. Adams farm accounts, Skaneateles, 1844-1850; and the John Hitchings Account Book in the Raymond Clark Hitchings Papers.

There were, in addition, innumerable church records and cemetery records at the Syracuse Public Library and the Onondaga Historical Association.

Census and Tax Records

The various published census reports were essential for this study. These include the following: *Aggregate Amount of Persons within the United States in the Year 1810* (Washington: n.p., 1811); *Census for 1820* (Washington: Gales and Seaton, 1821); *Fifth Census, or, Enumeration of the Inhabitants of the United States, 1830* (Washington: Duff Green, 1832); *Sixth Census or Enumeration of the Inhabitants of the United States, 1840* (Washington: Blair and Rives, 1841); *The Seventh Census of the United States: 1850* (Washington: Robert Armstrong, 1853); *Population of the United States in 1860; Compiled from the Original Returns of the Eighth Census* (Washington: U.S. Government Printing Office, 1864); *Digest of Accounts of Manufacturing Establishments in the United States and of Their Manufactures* (Washington: Gales and Seaton, 1823); "Census of the State of New York for the Year 1821," *Journal of the Assembly of New York,* 45th Session (Albany: n.p., 1822); "Census of the State of New York for the Year 1825," *Journal of the New York Senate,* 49th Session (Albany: n.p., 1826); *Census of the State of New-York, for 1835* (Albany: Croswell, VanBenthuysen & Burt, 1836); *Census of the State of New York, for 1845* (Albany: Carroll & Cook, 1846); *Census of the State of New York, for 1855* (Albany: Charles VanBenthuysen, 1857); and *Census of the State of New York, for 1865* (Albany: Charles VanBenthuysen & Sons, 1867). In addition, the manuscript schedules of the United States Census for 1810, 1820, 1830, 1840, 1850, and 1860 and the manuscript schedules of the New York State Census of 1855 were used to trace individuals. The agricultural and industrial schedules of the census of 1850 also provided valuable information. A description of census questionnaires and instructions to enumerators can be found in Carroll D. Wright, *The History and Growth of the United States Census* (Washington: U.S. Government Printing Office, 1900).

Tax records for various towns were available at the Syracuse Public Library and the Onondaga Historical Association, and in Bruce, *Onondaga's Centennial.* See also W. Freeman Galpin, compiler, "Early Records of the Village of Salina, New York" (typescript, 1957, Syracuse Public Library), and C. Edith Hall, compiler, "Early History and Records of the Town of Lysander" (typescript, 1935-1936, Syracuse Public Library).

INDEX

About the Author

Roberta Balstad Miller is a staff associate at the Social Science Research Council's Center for Coordination of Research on Social Indicators. Her essays have appeared in *Retrospective Technology Assessment 1976*, edited by Joel A. Tarr, and such journals as *Women's Studies* and *Historical Methods Newsletter.*